ACADEMIC'S

Questions Children Ask

John Bellingham

AIP

ACADEMIC (INDIA) PUBLISHERS

Published by :
ACADEMIC (INDIA) PUBLISHERS
B-9, Rattan Jyoti Building,
18, Rajendra Place
New Delhi-110008
Ph. : 5742171, 5812181
Fax : 91-11-5772171
E-mail : angelaip@del3.vsnl.net.in

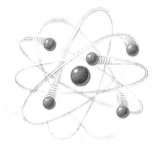

First Edition : 2001

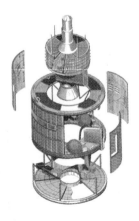

Price : Rs. 145.00 US $5

Printed at :
Haploos, Ph. : 549 8686

CONTENTS

1. THE UNIVERSE 1

2. THE SOLAR SYSTEM 9

3. THE EARTH 17

4. THE GREEN KINGDOM 23

5. THE ANIMAL KINGDOM 33

6. ENVIRONMENT 65

7. THE HUMAN BODY, HEALTH AND DISEASES 79

8. DISCOVERIES AND INVENTIONS 105

9. SCIENCE 119

10. OCEANS, CONTINENTS AND COUNTRIES 141

11. ANCIENT HISTORY 165

FLAGS OF SOME COUNTRIES

AFGHANISTAN

ARGENTINA

AUSTRALIA

AUSTRIA

BANGLADESH

BHUTAN

BRAZIL

CANADA

CHINA

CHILE

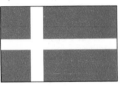

DENMARK

EGYPT

FRANCE

GERMANY

GREECE

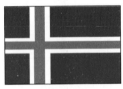

ICELAND

INDIA

INDONESIA

IRAN

IRAQ

JAPAN

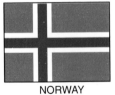

NORWAY

PAKISTAN

RUSSIA

SPAIN

SRI LANKA

UNITED KINGDOM

USA

UNIVERSE

Chapter 1

THE UNIVERSE

QUESTIONS

1. What does the Pulsating Theory of Evolution of the universe maintain?

2. What is the Big Bang theory?

3. What do the scientists think that the universe in the beginning was?

4. What does the universe consist of?

5. Our galaxy, the Milky Way contains about how many stars?

6. How many light years across is our galaxy, the Milky Way?

7. What holds the stars and galaxies together?

8. What is the shape of our galaxy, the Milky Way?

9. How many stars can be seen at a time, at night in the sky with the naked eye?

10. How many stars there might be in the universe?

11. Why does a star shine?

12. Why do stars twinkle?

BIG BANG

13. When does a star die and stop shining?

14. Which is the nearest star to the earth?

15. According to recent researches when did our Milky Way begin to form?

16. Which star does not move in the sky?

17. Which one of the stars is like our sun?

18. Among Cetus, Indus, Dorade and Hydra, which is the largest star?

19. Which of the planets is known as the Evening Star?

THE MILKY WAY

20. Why are observatories set high on mountains?

21. Sirius is the brightest star. Which other 2-stars are next to it in brightness?

22. If we watch the night sky long enough, the stars look moving from west to east. Why is it so?

23. One parsec shows the distance of how many light years?

24. When we look at a galaxy, which is 5 billion light years away from us, it means we are seeing this galaxy ....
....

25. Who began the systematic study of the sun, stars and the planets for the first time?

4-METRE TELESCOPE AT THE KITT PEAK NATIONAL OBSERVATORY

26. Who gave us the first comprehensive theory of the universe?

27. Who found a strong evidence in support of an ever expanding universe?

28. When was the famous Hubble space telescope launched?

29. Who was the first person to suggest that the earth is a sphere?

30. What is the brightness of a star called?

31. What is the colour of the large, hot and brilliant stars?

32. Why one would not get out of space?

33. Which nebula is the nearest to the earth?

34. In Greek mythology, of whose daughter is Andromeda mentioned as?

35. Which constellation is known as the Twins?

36. Castor is a beautiful double or binary star. What is its other partner?

37. In ancient greek mythology Castor and Pollux are described as brothers of whom?

38. What is the constellation Orion in Indian astronomy called?

39. What does the constellation Cancer mean?

40. The famous constellation Ursa Major is also known as the Great Bear, Hippopotamus, Plough and Dipper. By what name is it known in Indian astronomy?

41. The constellation Scorpius is quite familiar. It is also one of the Zodiacal signs. What is a super giant red star found in it called?

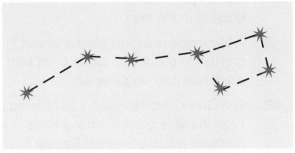

URSA MAJOR CONSTELLATION

CONSTELLATION CYGNUS

42. The constellation Cygnus, the Swan is called Hansa in Indian astronomy. According to Greek mythology a musician was changed into this constellation. What was his name?

43. The giant and biggest stars die and end up as what?

44. A Neutron Star may be just 15-20 km across and yet it may have as much matter as which of the other star?

45. Which constellation is popularly known as the Seven Sisters?

46. Argo used to be the name of a very huge and extensive constellation. But now it has been split up into four separate constellations called : 1. Carnia, the Keel; 2. Puppis, the Stern; 3. Vela, the Sail. What is the fourth part called?

47. What does Pysix signify?

48. Canis Minor is a constellaiton to the south of Gemini, the twins Castor and Pollux. Canis Minor means the Small Dog vis-a-vis Canis Major. What are these two dogs chasing in the sky?

49. A black hole is a most elusive object in the universe. It is a dead star with profound gravitation pull that it sucks even light which has the highest speed. Then how a black hole can be detected?

50. The Greek hero Hercules was ordered by the Oracle of Delphi to perform 12 Tasks. Later he was placed among stars and made a constellation. The constellation Hercules existing between Corona Borealis and Lyra can be seen performing some of these Twelve Tasks like killing the Lion (Leo), the Sea Snake (Hhdra), the crab (Cancer) etc. Who gave the Constellation Hercules this name?

51. Stars look as bright dots and are regarded as individuals. But many of them are really doublets, triplets, quaduplets etc. Some stars may be really clusters of so many stars that may count upto several hundred thousands. There is a cluster in Hercules. What is this cluster called?

52. What is cosmogony?

53. What is a Variable Star?

54. What is the luminosity of our galaxy the Milky Way?

55. What is the luminosity of the galaxy Andromeda (M-31)?

56. What type of galaxy is Pisces?

57. In which constellation is the bright star Eridanus?

58. What is the other or popular name of the constellation Canis Minor?

59. What is the Latin name of the constellation Twins?

60. What type of star is Arcturus found in the constellation Bootes.

61. Can you name the double stars of the constellation Great Bear, also called Ursa Major?

62. What shape is the galaxy Draco?

63. Of what shape are most of the local group of glaxies?

64. What is the possible diameter of the galaxy called Pegasus?

65. By whom was the names of the Zodiac given?

66. What is the popular name of the star Alpha Leonis?

67. How far is the star Procyon (Alpha Canis Minoris)?

68. What is the constellation Eagle called in Latin?

69. What is the constellaiton Lupus in English called?

70. The Latin name of a constellation is Pegasus. What is its English name?

71. In which constellaiton is Polaris?

Answers

1. The Pusating Theory of Evolution maintains that the Universe expands and contracts cyclically.

2. The Big Bang theory says that galaxies are moving away from one another at great speed.

3. Scientists believe that in the beginning the universe was many times smaller than even an atom.

4. The universe consists of the entire creation—the galaxies, the Milky Way, the stars, the sun, the earth and all that exists in the limitless space.

5. Our galaxy, the Milky Way contains about 200 billion stars.

6. Our galaxy, the Milky Way is 100,000 light years across.

7. The force and pull of gravity of the stars and galaxies exercised on one another holds them together.

8. The shape of our galaxy, the Milky Way is spiral.

9. About 6,000 stars can be seen at a time at night in the sky with the naked eye.

10. There might be about 200 billion stars in the universe.

SIDE VIEW OF MILKY WAY GALAXY

11. A star shines because there is continuous fusion of the atoms of hydrogen which in the process generate intense heat, energy and light.

12. The stars twinkle because they are too far way and their light bend after reaching the earth's atmosphere.

13. A star dies and stops shining when its supply of hydrogen gas is exhausted.

14. The nearest star to the Earth is Proxima centaurus.

15. Our Milky Way began to form about 10,000 million years ago.

16. Polaries does not move in the sky.

17. The star Tau Ceti is like our sun.

18. Hydra is the largest star of these.

19. Venus is known as the Evening Star.

20. Observatories are set high on mountains because the atmosphere there is clear and dry.

21. Canopus and Vega are next to Sirius in brightness.

22. If we watch the night sky long enough, the stars look moving from west to east because of the movement of the earth from east to west.

23. One parsec shows the distance of 3.26 light years.

24. When we look at a galaxy which is 5-billion light years away from us, it means we are seeing this galaxy as it was 5-billion years ago.

25. Babylonians began the systematic study of the sun, stars and the planets for the first time.

26. Ptolemy gave us the first comprehensive theory of the Universe.

27. Edwin Hubble found a strong evidence in support of an ever expanding universe.

28. The famous Hubble space Telescope was launched in 1990.

29. Pythagoras was the first person to suggest that the earth is a sphere.

30. The brightness of a star is called magnitude.

31. The large, hot and brilliant stars are red.

32. One would never get out of space because the path in the space is always curved.

33. The nebula Andromeda is the nearest to the earth.

34. In Greek mythology Andromeda is mentioned as the daughter of a king called Cepheus.

35. The constellation Gemini is known as the Twins.

36. The other partner of Castor is Pollux.

37. In ancient Greek mythology Castor and Pollux are described as brothers of Helen of Troy.

38. The constellation Orion in Indian astronomy is called Mriga.

39. The constellation Cancer means a crab.

40. The famous constellation Ursa Major is known as Saptarishi in Indian astronomy.

41. A super giant red star found in Scorpius is Antares.

42. It was the musician Orpheus who was changed into the constellaiton Cygnas, the Swan.

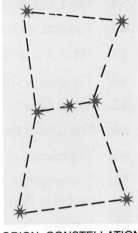

ORION CONSTELLATION

43. The giant and biggest stars die and end up as black holes.

44. A Neutron Star may be just 15-20 km across and yet it may have as much matter as the sun.

45. The constellation Pleiades is popularly known as the Seven Sisters.

46. The fourth part of Argo is called Pyxis.

47. Pysix signifies the Mariner's Compass.

48. Canis Major and Canis Minor, the two dogs are chasing the Mriga in the sky.

49. A black hole can be detected by observing its gravitational influence on the surroundings.

CONSTELLATION PLEIADES

50. The constellation Hercules was given its name by Eratosthenes.

51. The cluster found in the constellation Hercules is called M-13. M here stands for the French astronomer Messier who catalogued the Clusters.

52. Cosmogony means theory of the birth of the Universe.

53. A variable star is that which has variation of light because of periodic expansion or contraction.

54. The luminosity of our galaxy, the Milky Way is 15,000 million suns.

55. The luminosity of the galaxy Andromeda (M31) is 40,000 million suns.

56. The galaxy Pisces is irregular.

57. The bright star Eridamus is in the constellation Archernar.

58. The other or popular name of Canis Minor is the Little Dog.

59. The Latin name of the constellation Twins is Gemini

60. The star Arcturus found in the constellation Bootes is a Red giant.

61. Mizar and Alioth are the double stars of the constellation Great Bear.

62. The galaxy Draco is elliptical.

63. Most of the local groups of galaxies are either elliptical or irregular.

64. The galaxy Pegasus has the diameter of 7,000 light years.

65. The names of the Zodiac signs have been given by the Greeks.

66. The popular name of the star Alpha Leonis is Regulus.

67. The star Procyon is 11 light years away.

68. The constellation Eagle is called Aquila in Latin.

69. The constellation Lupus is called the Wolf in English.

70. The English name of the constellation Pegasus is Winged Horse.

71. Polaris is in the constellation Ursa Minor.

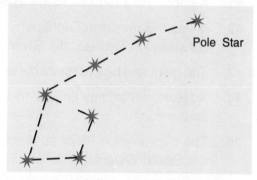

URSA MINOR CONSTELLATION

THE SOLAR SYSTEM

24. Which planet is called Enigmatic Planet?

25. Which planet is nearest to the Sun?

26. Which planet is visible only around sunrise or sunset?

27. Which is the only planet that rotates in a clockwise fashion?

28. The planet Mars rotates on its axis in almost the same period as is taken by the Earth. What is the exact time Mars takes in rotating on its axis?

29. Which is the fourth brightest object in the sky after the Sun, the Moon and the planet Venus?

30. In how many years does Saturn take a round of the Sun?

31. How many moons or satellites has the Saturn?

SATURN

32. Why does the planet Neptune appear blue in colour?

33. Which planet like the Earth has only one Moon or satellite?

34. Besides Saturn and Neptune which other planet has rings?

35. Why is the sun at the centre of the Solar System?

36. The sun is also a star, Why?

37. The energy of the sun sustains life on the earth. What is the sunlight (energy) received and trapped by plants and animals called?

38. Why Saturn is the most spectacular of all the planets?

39. It is highly dangerous to look directly at the sun. How do astronomers observe it?

40. The sun was born out of a nebula—a huge cloud of gas and dust. What became of the leftover material after the sun was formed?

41. The sunlight reaches the earth in about eight minutes travelling 147,100,000 km. How much time does it take to reach the planet Jupiter which is 778,300,000 km away from the sun?

42. What is the instrument used to study and investigate the light of the sun?

43. Substances like water, oxygen, carbon etc. make life possible and sustainable on the earth. These are continually re-cycled. What helps these recycles the most?

44. Which is the smallest planet in our solar system?

45. What is the Zodiac?

46. Who discovered the outer-most planet Pluto?

47. The moon is just 1/81 of the weight of the earth. How much gravity it has?

48. What is a constellation?

49. On which planet can be found large canyons, larger than the American Grand Canyon?

50. How huge is the largest Martian canyon called Olympus Mons?

51. What are the number of known moons of Neptune?

52. Which comet hit Jupiter in July 1994?

53. How many moons has Saturn?

54. The planet Mars has two moons. One is Phobos, what is other?

55. The planet Pluto has only one satellite or moon. What is it called?

56. Janus is the Moon of which Planet?

57. Which of the Moons is the nearest to Jupiter

58. What is the axial tilt of Mars?

59. What is the duration of day on Saturn?

60. What is the orbital period of Venus?

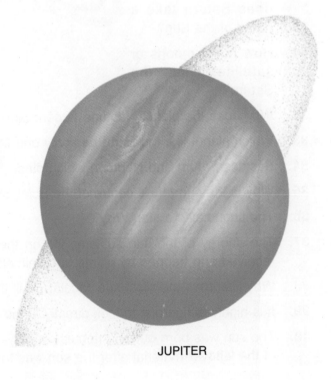

JUPITER

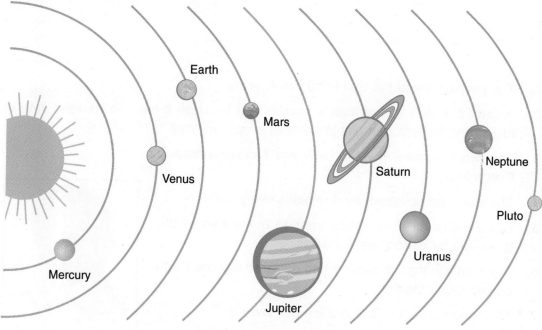

OUR SOLAR SYSTEM

61. What is the equatorial diameter of Uranus?

62. What is the average surface temperature of Pluto?

63. Which other planet besides Pluto has the average temperature of -220°C.

64. What is the average distance of Mars from the Sun?

65. What is the maximum apparent magnitude of Jupiter?

66. Which comet takes the longest time to make one round of the Sun?

67. How much time does the Halley's Comet take in making a round of the sun?

68. What is the Sun's polar rotation period?

69. Which is larger Mercury or Venus?

70. Which planet is of the same size as that of the moon?

HALLEY'S COMET

71. Of what largely is composed the atmosphere of Venus?

1. The possible life of the Sun is 10 billion years.

2. A giant star dies earlier than a smaller one becuase there is a massive rate of fusion and its hydrogen gas is spent at a very fast rate.

3. The two branches of Astronomy are Astrophysics and Cosmology.

4. The stars rise up earlier by 4 minutes every night.

5. Galileo was the first astronomer to make use of the telescope for astronomical studies.

6. Aryabhatta in the 5th century had declared that the Earth orbited round the sun.

7. The speed of light is 299,792 km per second.

8. The brightest star Sirius in the constellation Canis Major is 8.7 light years far from us.

GALILEO GALILIE

9. The Sputnik 1 was launched by the Soviet Union on October 4, 1957.

10. Neil Armstrong was the first astronaut to set his foot on the Moon.

11. The spaceship Voyager 2 launched by the US visited four planets, Jupiter, Saturn, Uranus and Neptune.

12. Pathfinder landed on Mars on 4th July, 1997.

13. There are nine planets in the Solar System.

14. The Sun is mainly made up of hydrogen.

15. The surface temperature of the Sun is 6,000°C.

16. 500 million tonnes of hydrogen is being turned into helium every second in the nuclear fusion on the Sun.

17. The sunspots attain a peak in about 11 years.

18. The Solar Prominences shoot to the height of about 10,000 km at times.

19. The corona of the sun can be seen during a solar eclipse.

CORONA OF THE SUN

20. A solar eclipse takes place on the new moon day when the moon comes directly in front of the sun.

21. The sun has spent almost half of its life so far.

22. The sun's centripetal gravity prevents the planets etc. in the solar system moving off in a straight line into space.

23. Mercury, Venus, Earth and Mars are the planets known as the Inner Planets.

24. Pluto is called the Enigmatic Planet.

25. Mercury is the nearest planet to the sun.

26. Venus is visible only around sunrise or sunset.

27. Venus is the only planet that rotates in a clockwise fashion.

28. Mars takes 24 hours 37 minutes in rotating on its axis.

29. Jupiter is the fourth brightest planet in the sky.

30. Saturn takes a round of the Sun in 30 years.

31. Saturn has 18 moons or the satellites.

32. The planet Neptune appears blue in colour because of the methane gas on it.

33. The planet Neptune has only one moon or satellite like the Earth.

34. Besides Saturn and Neptune, Jupiter has rings.

35. The sun is at the centre of the Solar System because the mass of the sun is greater than the combined mass of all the planets.

36. The sun is also a star because of its nuclear reaction at its core that creates so much heat and pressure.

37. The sunlight (energy) received and trapped by plants and animals is called biomass.

38. Saturn is most spectacular of all the planets becuase of its colured rings.

39. The astronomers look at the sun by projecting its image on to a surface or photographic film.

40. The leftover of the nebula, after the birth of the sun, became planets and asteroids.

41. The sunlight takes 43 minutes to reach Jupiter.

42. The instrument used to study and investigate the light of the sun is spectrometer.

43. Energy from the sun helps most in the recycles of water, oxygen, carbon etc.

44. Pluto is the smallest planet in our solar system.

45. The part of the sky through which the sun, the moon, the earth and other planets travel is called the Zodiac.

46. The outermost planet Pluto was discovered by Tombaugh.

47. The moon's gravity is one-sixth that of the earth.

48. A group of stars which makes a familiar pattern of an animal, man, alphabet or figure is a constellation.

49. Large canyons, larger than the American Grand Canyon can be found on Mars.

50. The largest Martian canyon Olympus Mons is 25 km high.

51. The number of known moons of Neptune is 8.

52. The comet Shoemaker Levy hit Jupiter in July 1994.

53. Saturn has 18 moons.

54. The other moon of Mars besides Phobos is Deimos.

55. The planet Pluto's moon is called Charon.

56. Janus is the moon of Saturn.

57. Metis is the nearest moon to Jupiter.

58. The axial tilt of Mars is 24°.

59. The duration of day on Saturn is 17.23 hours.

60. The orbital period of Venus is 224.7 days.

61. The equatorial diameter of Uranus is 51,118 km.

URANUS

62. The average surface temperature of Pluto is -220°C.

63. The other planet besides Pluto to have -220°C temperature is Neptune.

64. The average distance of Mars from the sun is 227.9 million km.

65. The maximum apparent magnitude of Jupiter is -2.8.

66. Great comet of 1843 takes the longest time to make one round of the sun.

67. Halley's Comet takes 76.3 years to make one round of the sun.

68. The sun's polar rotation period is 35 days.

69. Venus is larger than Mercury.

70. Mercury is of the same size as that of the moon.

71. The atmosphere of Venus is largely composed of carbon dioxide and clouds of sulphuric acid.

THE EARTH

Chapter 3

THE EARTH

*Q*UESTIONS

1. How old is the Earth?
2. What is the equatorial diameter of the Earth?
3. What is the temperature of the inner core at the very centre of the Earth?
4. How much of the Earth's surface is covered with oceans and seas?

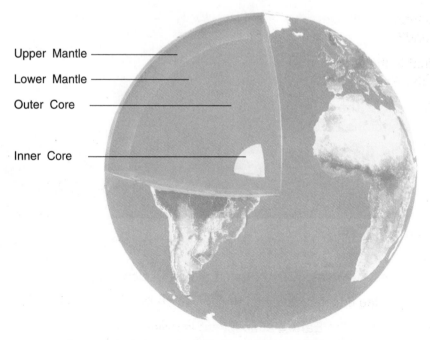

Upper Mantle ——————

Lower Mantle ——————

Outer Core ——————

Inner Core ——————

EARTH CUTAWAY SHOWING INTERNAL STRUCTURE

5. The famous Colorado Grand Canyon is at places one and half km deep and how much wide?

6. How much is the inclination of the Earth to the plane?

7. Which are the two days when day and night are of equal duration, that is 12 hours each?

8. Why there is no life on other planets?

9. Fair weather is associated with which type of pressure?

10. What type of pressure results in storms, torrential rains and hurricanes?

11. Which is the second brightest object in the sky?

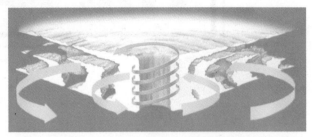

HURRICANE : THE DAMP AIR RISES HIGHER AND CONDENSES INTO THICK CLOUDS. THEY ARE BLOWN INTO A SPIRAL BY THE WIND.

12. Why is there no solar eclipse on every new moon day and lunar eclipse on every full moon day?

13. Why do earthquakes occur?

14. What is a glacier?

15. Where can the continental glaciers be found?

16. What is the surface area of the Earth?

17. What is the polar diameter of the Earth?

18. What is the average surface temperature of the Earth?

19. When and who discovered the Ozone layer?

A BUILDING DAMAGED BY AN EARTHQUAKE

20. What does Meteorology, the branch of earth-science study?

21. When did the first microscopic forms of life on the Earth is said to have appeared?

22. Which layer of the Earth's atmosphere is called Troposphere?

23. An object that orbits a planet is called a satellite. What is a natural satellite called?

24. When was the far side of the Moon for the first time photographed by a Russian space-probe?

25. What is the dust that covers the surface of the moon called?

26. The surface of the moon looks pock-marked because of its numberless craters. How most of these were formed?

27. How much time does Moon take to revolve once round the Earth?

28. Why is there the full Moon?

29. The surface of the Earth is about 40 km thick on average. We all stand and walk on it and perform all other activities. What is it called?

30. When do high tides in our seas and oceans occur?

31. What is a lunar month?

32. How far does the Earth's atmosphere stretch from its surface?

33. The thick cover of the atmosphere around the earth has as many as seven layers of gases. What is the farthest layer called?

34. Why is it cold in winter and hot in summer?

35. The earth is rotating round the sun. But why we do not feel this motion?

36. Do all other planets revolve round the sun?

37. What is the axis of the earth?

38. When it is winter in the northern hemisphere, what is there in the southern hemisphere?

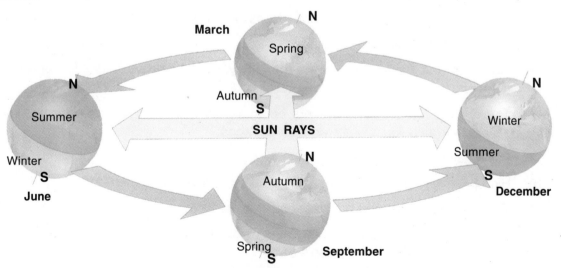

SEASONS AT DIFFERENT TIMES OF THE YEAR

39. Is the shape of the earth's orbit circular or elliptical?

40. What is at the centre of the earth?

41. What should be the speed of a rocket to counter earth's gravity and rise up into the atmosphere?

42. What should be the speed of a rocket to escape from the earth's gravitation into the outer space?

43. Air has weight and pressure. Why do we not feel the pressure?

44. How much is atmospheric pressure in general?

45. What is climatology?

46. What is continental drift?

47. What would happen if the moon's orbit was on the same plane as that of the earth?

$\mathcal{A}$NSWERS

1. The earth is about 5,000 million years old.

2. The equatorial diameter of the Earth is 12,756 km.

3. The temperature of the inner core at the very centre of the earth is 7,000°C.

4. Seventy percent of the earth's surface is covered with oceans and seas.

5. The famous Colorado Canyon is at places one and half km deep and 29 km wide.

6. The earth's inclination to the plane is 23.5°.

7. March 21 and September 22 are the 2 days when day and night are of equal duration.

8. There is no life on other planets because they do not have oxygen in their atmosphere and liquid water on their surfaces.

9. Fair weather is associated with low pressure.

10. High pressure results in storms, torrential rains and hurricanes.

11. The moon is the second brightest object in the sky.

12. There is no solar eclipse on every new moon day and lunar eclipse on every full moon day becuase of the moon's 5° tilt.

13. Earthquakes occur because of the movement of the gigantic plates which rumble and clash at times.

14. A slow and moving mass of ice and snow on land is a glacier.

15. Continental glaciers can be found on Antarctica and Greenland.

16. The surface area of the Earth is about 510 million sq. km.

17. The polar diameter of the Earth is 12,714 km.

18. The average surface temperature of the Earth is 15°C.

19. Charls Fabryalis discovered the Ozone Layer in 1913.

GLACIER

20. Meteorology is the branch of earth-science that studies weather.

21. The first microscopic forms of life is said to have appeared 3,600 million years ago.

22. The lowest layer of the earth's atmosphere is called Troposphere.

23. A natural satellite is called the moon.

24. The far side of the moon was for the first time photographed by a Russian space probe in 1959.

25. The dust that covers the surface of the moon is called regolith.

THERMOSPHERE

MESOSPHERE

STRATOSPHERE

TROPOSPHERE

26. The surface of the moon looks pock-marked becuase of its numberless craters. Most of these were formed by meteorite bombardments.

LAYERS OF THE EARTH'S ATMOSPHERE

27. The moon revolves round the earth once in 27 days and 8 hours.

28. There is full moon because then the earth is between the sun and the moon and its side facing the earth is fully illuminated.

29. The surface of the earth is called the crust.

30. High tides in our seas and oceans occur when the sun and moon line up and pull the waters on the earth in the same direction.

31. The time between the 2 fullmoons is called a lunar month.

32. The earth's atmosphere stretch upto 1000 km from its surface.

33. The farthest layer of the atmosphere around the earth is called exosphere.

34. It is cold in winter and hot in summer because of the position of the earth's axis in respect of the sun.

35. The earth is rotating round the sun but we do not feel this motion becuase we also move along with the earth's surface as it moves with its whole atmosphere.

36. Yes, all other planets revolve round the sun.

37. An imaginary line that runs through the earth from the North to the South Pole.

38. When it is winter in the northern hemisphere it is summer in the southern hemisphere.

39. The shape of the earth's orbit is elliptical.

40. At the centre of the earth is solid metal.

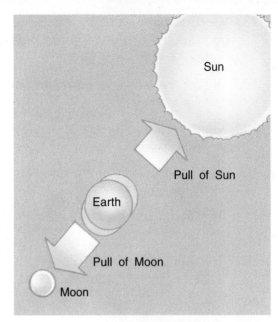

HIGH TIDES

EARTH'S AXIS

41. In order to counter earth's gravity and rise up into the atmosphere, a rocket should have minimum speed of 8 km per second.

42. A rocket should have the speed of 11km per second to escape from the earth's gravitation into the outer space.

43. We do not feel the pressure of the air because there is an equal pressure inside our body.

44. The atmospheric pressure in general is 14 1/2 lb per square inch.

45. Climatology is the study of climate of the earth and its distribution.

46. Continental drift is the process by which one or more landmasses split apart and drifted literally to form the present day continents.

47. If the moon's orbit was on the same plane as that of the earth then there would be lunar eclipse every month.

THE GREEN KINGDOM

Chapter 4

THE GREEN KINGDOM

SOME KINDS OF SEEDS

QUESTIONS

1. What is a seed?

2. What is inside a seed?

3. What makes the right conditions for a seed to grow?

4. How do flowers produce seeds?

5. Who makes food for the plant?

6. Besides sending up sap and minerals, what other functions do roots perform?

7. What is the process of changing light energy into chemical energy in the plants, called?

8. Which carbohydrates are produced in the plants through photosynthesis?

9. Which main pigment is found in green and living leaves?

10. What is released as a waste product by trees and plants?

11. Plants are 'phototropic. What is phototropism?

12. What is the name of the substance that is responsible for bending of plants towards sunlight or some other stimulus?

13. Why is a leaf green?

14. Besides chlorophyll which other pigments are found in leaves?

15. What is the abscission zone?

16. What are deciduous trees?

17. Why do leaves on dead branches do not fall?

18. Why the leaves of some trees never change colours?

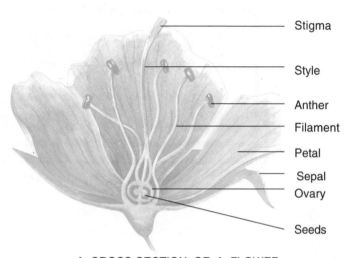

A CROSS-SECTION OF A FLOWER

19. What type of leaves have the ever green trees?

20. What is a flower? What is its main function?

21. What is the female part of a flower called?

22. What are stamens?

23. What are ephemerals?

24. What is nectar?

25. What attracts bees and birds to flowers?

26. What is anther? What is its function?

27. Chrysanthemums are perennials or ephemerals.

28. How long do the biennials live?

29. What are the plants, that complete their life-cycle in one year, called?

30. What is one of the many useful functions of plants?

31. Which gas is used by plants as a raw material in photosynthesis?

32. Who was the first botanist?

33. Which book of Darwin has deeply influenced the classification of animals and plants?

34. Who discovered the laws of genetics?

35. Who laid the foundation of modern biochemistry?

BIENNIAL PLANT

36. Who coined the term Ecology?

37. How can you tell the age of a tree?

38. Of what is the bark of a tree mainly made up?

39. Why do cacti have spines?

40. How are seeds spread and scattered by birds and animals?

41. What is the life science?

42. What is the study of how living organisms react and relate to one another and to their environment, is called?

43. Plants and trees have different kinds of cells with their own particular function. Xylem cells carry water and mineral salts from the roots to the other parts of a plant. What do the epidermal cells do?

44. What are spores?

45. What are lichens?

46. What is symbiotic relation?

47. What is a mushroom?

48. Are mosses plants or animals?

49. What are the two types of cones borne by conifers?

50. Conifers are cone-bearing evergreen trees. They are some of the oldest plans and include ....

51. Which plants are called amphibians?

52. What are insectivorous plants?

53. What is a cash crop?

54. What is herbalism?

55. What type of herb is ginger?

56. How firs protect themselves from frost and snow?

57. Why plants attract insects?

58. What are xerophyte plants?

59. How xerophytes escape drought and scarcity of water?

60. What are truffles?

61. How truffles are found?

62. What is the difference between fruits and vegetables?

63. Where did the orange originate?

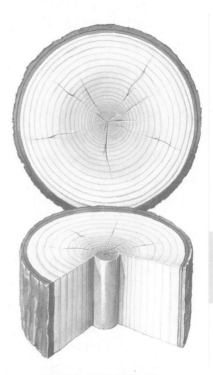

CROSS SECTION OF A TREE TRUNK

FLY AGARIC — A POISONOUS VARIETY

64. Which is the tallest tree?

65. How is seaweed useful?

66. Is bamboo a grass?

67. What is a banayana tree?

68. How does a coconut grow?

69. What is a greenhouse?

70. Why bananas are harvested green?

71. Is the cucumber a fruit or a vegetable?

72. What is the oldest and premier table fruit of the world?

73. What is biota?

74. Of what colour is poppy?

75. What is the Latin name of the flowering plant Sweet William?

76. What is daisy called in Latin?

77. What are weeds?

78. What is the popular name of hibiscus?

79. The violet (viola) is annual or perennial?

80. What is the proximate maximum height of birch?

81. What is the common name of laburnum?

82. What is the popular name of Mangifera indica?

83. Apple belongs to the family of Rosaceae. To which family does pear belong to?

84. What is an aerial root?

THE GLASS WALLS OF A GREENHOUSE

AERIAL ROOT

ANSWERS

1. A seed is a tiny structure and capsule of life.

2. The seed contains food and a very tiny plant.

3. The right conditions for a seed to grow are proper soil, warmth, adequate moisture and oxygen.

4. Flowers produce seeds through the process of pollination and fertilization.

5. Leaves make food for the plant from sunlight, air and water.

6. Roots keep a plant steady and erect and act like a strong base and foundation.

7. It is called photosynthesis.

8. Glucose, sucrose and starch.

9. Chlorophyll.

10. Oxygen.

11. Phototropism is the bending or turning of plants to a stimulus of external light.

12. The substance is called auxins.

13. Because of the pre-dominance of chlorophyll, a green pigment.

14. Other pigments besides chlorophyll are carotenes (orange) and xenthophyll (red/yellow).

15. It is formation of a thin layer of cork at the base of the petiole or stalk that attaches the leaf to the stem.

16 Deciduous trees are those that shed their leaves in autumn.

17. Leaves on dead branches do not fall because of absence of the formation of an abscission zone.

18. The leaves of some trees do not change colour because they are evergreen trees and do not shed their leaves.

19. Evergreen trees have tough leathery leaves that range from needles to scales. They do not allow the loss of water.

20. A flower is a reproductive structure and its main function is to produce seeds.

21. The female part of a flower is called stigma.

22. Stamens are male parts of a flower.

23. These are the plants that live for a short period and then die in the same season.

24. Nectar is a sweet juice or substance found in flowers which birds and insects use as food.

ROOTS OF A PLANT

PHOTOTROPISM

25. The bright colours and sweet smell of the flowers attract bees and birds to them.

HONEY BEE SUCKING
HONEY FROM A FLOWER

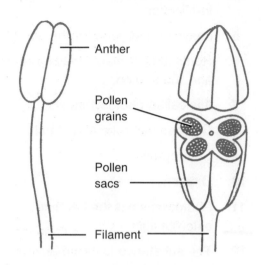

STRUCTURE OF ANTHER

26. An anther is the head of a stamen. The function of anther is to produce pollens, the male germ cells.

27. Chrysanthemums are perennials because they live for many years.

28. Biennial plants live for the duration of two years.

29. Plants that complete their life-cycle in one year, are called annuals.

30. One of the many useful functions of plants is to produce oxygen.

31. Plants use carbon dioxide as a raw material in photosynthesis.

32. Greek thinker Theophrastus was the first botanist.

33. Charles Darwin's book The Origin of Species deeply influenced the classification of animals and plants.

34. Gregor Mendel discovered the laws of genetics for the first time.

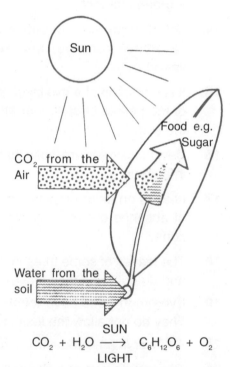

$$CO_2 + H_2O \xrightarrow[\text{LIGHT}]{\text{SUN}} C_6H_{12}O_6 + O_2$$

PROCESS OF PHOTOSYNTHESIS

35. Claude Bernard laid the foundation of modern bio-chemistry.

36. The term Ecology was coined by a German scientist Ernst Haeckel.

37. We can tell the age of a tree by counting the rings found in the cross-section of a tree-trunk.

38. The bark of a tree is mainly made up of cork.

39. A cactus is a wonderful plant that grows in arid and hot areas. The water is stored in it for use in drier and more hot season in the spongy hollow stem. Cacti have spines that help them prevent the loss of water. They also protect cacti from being eaten by thirsty animals.

40. Birds and animals eat the juicy fruits containing seeds and then spit the seeds here and there. They may travel miles and miles and then drop them in the form of their solid waste. Some seeds are sticky and have hooks, so they catch on to the hair and furs of the animals to be brushed off later in distant places.

41. The life science is the science and study of living beings or organisms.

42. Ecology.

43. Epidermal cells store food for the plants and trees.

44. A spore is a unicellular asexual reproductive unit found in algae and fungi. They are of many different types.

45. Lichens are plants composed of both algal and fungal cells in symbiotic association. They secrete organic acids which can erode rocks to provide them mineral nutrition.

LICHENS

46. Symbiotic relation is a type of mutualism between two organisms of different types. In this relation both interacting organisms benefit multually. They live in harmoney with each other.

47. A mushroom is an umbrella-like fruiting body of a fungi.

48. Mosses are plants : They are very small and simple plants which grow in clumps in damp conditions. They are of hundreds of species.

49. Conifers bear male and female cones. Male cones are small and produce pollen. This pollen is carried to large female cones by winds where it fertilizers the eggs which in due course of time become seeds.

FIELD MUSHROOM — A
NUTRITIOUS VEGETARIAN FOOD

50. Pines, cypresses, cedars, yews, larches and redwoods.

51. An amphibian organism is one that can live and survive both in water and on land. Mosses and liverworts are amphibian plants. They can live without water for a long time but need to remain underwater to grow new plants.

52. Insectivorous or carnivorous plants obtain their food both by trapping, killing and digesting small creatures and normal photosynthesis.

53. A cash crop is that which is grown mainly not for food for the family but to be sold for money in the market. Coffee, tea, jute, sugar, tobacco etc. are some good examples of cash crops.

PINE LEAF

54. Any plant used as a medicine, seasoning or flavouring is call a herb. For example, mint, thyme, basil and sage are herbs. Growing and cultivation of such plants is called herbalism.

55. Ginger is a very useful culinary herb. It is used both in dry and fresh forms. It is used as spice and herb for flavouring dishes and also as a medicine. It is obtained from a tall grasslike plant. Ginger is harvested after flowering.

COFFEE PLANT (A CASH CROP)

56. When there is heavy frost and snowfall in winter, the fir trees bend their branches and the snow slides off.

57. Plants attract insects because they help plants in pollination. Plants have sweet smelling and colourful flowers which attract and invite insects.

58. Xerophyte plants are those that can survive in conditions of water deficiency. They can endure and resist droughts.

59. Xerophytes spread their roots horizontally so as to soak up whatever water is available on the surface of the soil. Some xerophytes strike deep roots to reach deep down the damp places.

60. Truffle is a kind of fungus that grows 5-10 cm below the ground. They resemble tubers and many of them are edible.

61. Truffles have peculiar smell and grow 5-10 cm below the ground. Pigs and dogs are used to find and dig out truffles. They can sniff truffles and then dig them out with their snout or paws.

62. Technically any fleshy part of a plant comes under the category of fruit that has seeds and developed from a flower. Thus, besides apples, organges, mangoes etc. beans and peas are fruits. Any plant that has a soft stem or no, or less woody tissues is a vegetable. Thus melons, pumpkins, tomatoes etc. are vegetables though they have seeds and develop from flowers.

63. Nobody knows for sure where the oranges originated. But it is said that this fruit spread to other countries from India.

64. Trees are the tallest and oldest of living things. Some of the trees are over 4000 years old. The redwood trees found in California, USA are the known and living tallest trees. A few of these may be as tall as 110 metres.

65. Seaweed is of many kinds. It is a microscopic, marine algae found in seas and oceans. They are used

SEAWEEDS

as food and fertilizers. Smaller marine creatures feed on seaweed. Seaweed also gives off oxygen and thereby helps the waters to remain clean and pure.

66. Yes, bamboo is a grass, a great grass, however it looks like a tree or a bush. It can grow at a rate of 41 cm per day. It can reach upto 36 mt height.

67. The banyan tree is as wonderful as it is giant. It is of mulberry family and is found in India and Malaysia. Its big and heavy branches spread all around its trunk. These branches send down roots to the ground which grow into many new roots.

68. The coconut is a tall palm tree grown along the coastal region. It has hard dark shell with three eyes which are actually its buds. When a coconut is planted, a new sprout comes out of one of these eyes and a new palm is grown.

BANYAN TREE

31

69. A greenhouse is a glass-structure in which plants, vegetables and flowers can be grown all the year round.

70. Bananas are harvested while they are green in order to prolong their shelf-life. If bananas are harvested when ripe and yellow, they would soon start rotting. Moreover, a banana that is allowed to ripen on the plant would lose its flovour.

71. The cucumber is both a fruit and a vegetable.

72. The honour of being the oldest and premier table fruit of the world goes to the apple.

73. The flora and fauna of a particular area, or a particular geological period is called biota.

74. Poppy is red, pink or white.

75. The Latin name of Sweet Williams is dianthus.

76. Daisy is called bellis in Latin.

POPPY FLOWER

77. Weeds or rogues are plants that are different from rest of the crop and so unwanted. For example, wild oat growing in a cultivated field is a weed. Removal and eradication of unwanted plants is called weeding. Thistles, nettles, common couch grass, goose foot etc. are weeds.

78. The popular name of hibiscus is the flower of an hour.

79. The violet is an annual plant.

80. The proximate maximum height of birch is 10 mt.

81. The common name of laburnum is golden rain.

82. The popular name of Mangifera Indica is mango.

83. Pear also belongs to the family of Rosaceae.

84. An aerial root arises from the shoot of a plant, or tree outside the ground. It helps in absorption of water from humid air.

BIRCH TREE (BETULA)

THE ANIMAL KINGDOM

Chapter 5

THE ANIMAL KINGDOM

QUESTIONS

1. What is the approximate number of different kinds of animals?
2. What percentage of animals are vertebrates?
3. What is the one major difference between animals and plants?
4. How do animals procreate?
5. What is biology?
6. What are the main divisions of Biology?
7. Who discovered the laws of genetics and when?
8. What determines and controls our character and traits?
9. What is evolution?
10. What is the simplest form from which life has emerged?
11. Who propounded the Theory of Evolution?
12. On what is the Theory of Evolution based?
13. What does the Theory of Evolution say in brief?
14. About how many kinds of mammals are there?

SEAL (A MAMMAL)

15. Where is milk produced in the female mammals?

16. What insulates the mammals?

17. Why are mammals called placental?

18. Mammals have a bony skeleton in which the backbone forms the main body axis. What are the other vital organs they have in common?

19. What is gestation?

20. What are primates?

21. Which animal is the biggest of the primates?

22. Where are lions found now?

23. What is a 'pride'?

24. Which land animal is the fastest? What can be its maximum speed?

BIG CAT

25. Why are there stripes or spots on the skin of big cats?

26. Who has written a beautiful poem on the tiger beginning with the words: "Tiger! Tiger! burning bright?"

27. What do marsupial mammals mean?

28. What is the size of a newborn baby kangaroo?

29. How much can a kangaroo jump up to?

30. Where are tree-dwelling small mammal opossums found?

31. Which mammals live in the sea?

32. Which are the largest animals?

33. Which sea mammals are believed to have an elaborate language?

34. What is blubber?

35. Which sea mammals are amphibians?

36. Which sea mammal has tusks?

37. Long long ago some very huge and giant animals roamed all over the earth. But later they perished and disappeared. Which living animal is their descendant?

38. What was a mammoth?

39. How tall is an elephant?

40. What is the elephant's most remarkable organ?

BONES OF MAMMOTH FOUND PRESERVED IN THE EARTH

41. What has been the source of the elephant's undoing?

42. How many elephants there might be left now all over the world?

43. What is a 'finger' that an elephant has? How many 'fingers' does the African elephant have?

44. How long does an Asian elephant live?

45. How many different kinds of birds of prey are there?

46. How does the sparrow hawk hunt?

47. What makes the birds so light and worthy of flying?

48. From what kind of animals have birds evolved?

49. What is moulting?

50. How do birds eat their food in the absence of teeth?

51. What is protective colouration?

52. Which is the largest living flightless bird?

53. Kiwis are another flightless birds. Where are they found?

KIWI

54. Which is the favourite haunt of penguins? At which other places are penguins found?

55. Penguins are flightless sea birds. Why did their wings change into flippers?

56. How many kinds of penguins are there? Which is the biggest penguin?

57. What do owl feed on?

58. Why can an owl see at night?

59. What makes the owl to swoop down stealthily right on its prey?

60. Can owls hear?

61. How does the owl eat its prey?

62. Which is the only mammal that can fly?

63. Which are the two major classes of bats?

64. What is echolocation?

65. Which bat feeds on blood?

66. How does a bat sit on a tree?

67. What is migration of birds?

68. Why do birds migrate?

69. The Arctic tern completes a journey of about how many miles both ways during migration?

70. How do birds find their path and reach their destination of migration?

ARCTIC TERN

71. How many kinds of snakes are there?

72. Which is the largest snake?

73. How does a python kill its prey.

74. Which are the other large snakes besides the python?

75. Which is the deadliest snake?

76. Which snake can dilate its neck into a hood?

77. What is a rattlesnake?

78. How does a rattlesnake's tail begin to rattle?

79. Most snakes lay eggs. How do snake hatchings break through the egg?

80. Which snake does not lay eggs?

81. What are crocodilians?

82. Where are crocodilians found?

83. How do they kill their victims?

84. How would you distinguish an alligator from a crocodile?

85. Which one major purpose does colouring in animals serve?

86. What are arborial lizards?

CROCODILE

87. How does the chameleon change its colours?

88. What results in yellow colouring and spots in a chameleon?

89. Why do tortoises and turtles need not run?

90. How do turtles and tortoises catch insects to feed on?

91. How many different kinds of lizards are there?

92. Do the lizards hibernate in winter?

93. Which is the flying lizard?

94. Which lizards feed on ants?

95. When did creatures like jelly-fish and sponges evolve?

96. When did the Age of Dinosaurs begin?

97. When did the dinosaurs become extinct?

98. From which common ancestor are birds supposed to have evolved?

99. What does the extinction of dinosaurs prove?

100. What are cartilaginous animals?

101. Upto what maximum length can a shark grow?

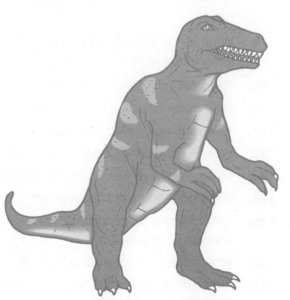

ALLOSAURUS DINOSAURS

102. Why are some sharks dangerous?

103. How does a ray differ from a shark?

104. Why some sharks follow a ship? What are these sharks called?

105. How do fish absorb oxygen?

106. Can a fish hear, smell and taste?

107. Which are the fish that can live out of water.

108. Why sometimes fish come out on the surface of water and try to breathe in air?

109. Which is the largest living animal?

110. What makes a fish a perfect swimmer?

111. How does colouring help the fish?

112. Majority of the fish belong to which category?

113. Where are the organs of smell located in the fish?

114. How do frogs and tadpoles breathe?

115. Can frogs live without breathing?

116. What is the popular superstition about salamanders?

117. What are newts? What is the "breeding dress" of the great-crested newt?

SALAMANDER

118. What is the number of eggs that a female frog lays?

119. Tadpoles have tails. What happens to their tails when they become adult frogs?

120. How much time does a frog take in developing from an egg to an adult frog?

121. How long can a frog or toad live?

122. What distinguishes frogs from toads?

123. Can some frogs live on trees? How do they live there?

124. What does the word "amphibian" mean? Which are the amphibian animals?

125. What is the approximate number of different species of amphibians?

126. What is strange about the midwife male toad?

127. Which frog keeps its eggs in a sack under its throat?

128. Which frog lays its eggs in a nest?

129. What is a virus?

TOAD

130. How viruses destroy cells of a host animal or plant?

131. What are bacteria?

132. What is the difference between butterflies and moths?

133. What is the known number of different species of butterflies?

134. What are the different stages of change through which the butterfly passes to become an adult butterfly?

135. Can the butterflies and moths smell?

136. How are ladybirds friends of farmers?

137. When was bacteria discovered and by whom?

138. How do bacteria reproduce?

139. What are the four categories of bacteria?

140. What is infection?

141. How is malaria caused?

142. How many different kinds of bacteria are there?

143. How do bacteria help in digestion in animals and men?

144. What is nitrogen-fixation? How do bacteria help in it?

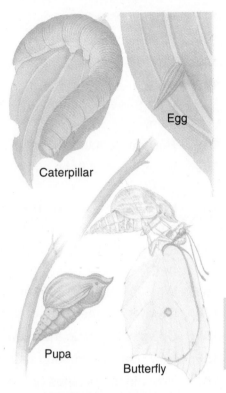

Egg

Caterpillar

Pupa

Butterfly

DIFFERENT STAGES OF DEVELOPMENT IN BUTTERFLY

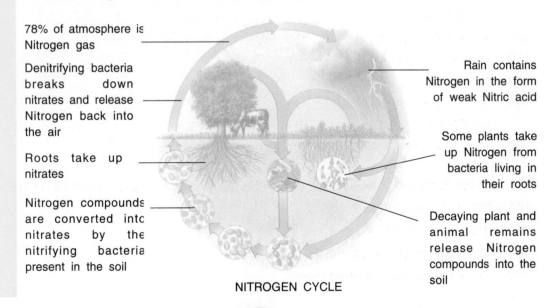

78% of atmosphere is Nitrogen gas

Denitrifying bacteria breaks down nitrates and release Nitrogen back into the air

Roots take up nitrates

Nitrogen compounds are converted into nitrates by the nitrifying bacteria present in the soil

Rain contains Nitrogen in the form of weak Nitric acid

Some plants take up Nitrogen from bacteria living in their roots

Decaying plant and animal remains release Nitrogen compounds into the soil

NITROGEN CYCLE

145. What is chitin?

146. What is moulting?

147. How are an insect's eyes wonderful?

148. How many different known and recognised species of insects are there?

149. How do insects feel, smell and hear?

150. What types of bees can be found in a hive?

151. What is the job of the queen bee among the honey bees?

152. How there is only one queen bee in a hive?

153. What is the job of worker bees?

154. Of what are the webs of spiders made ?

155. Do spiders eat up their own webs?

156. How does an amoeba reproduce?

157. How did the octopus get its name?

158. How does the octopus escape from its predators?

159. Is the octopus able to change its colours? Why does he do so?

160. Of what use are the tentacles to a jellyfish?

161. What are polyps?

162. How vast is a coral reef?

163. What is a coral atoll?

164. Why is lobster called a decapod?

165. How many eggs can a female lobster lay?

166. In the first year of its existence how many times does lobster shed its hard shell?

167. What is a laughing hyena?

168. Do fishes smell?

169. What are viviparous fishes?

170. Do fishes weep and shed tears?

OCTOPUS

POLYPS

171. Why does a snake swing its body sideways into curves or loops?

172. Why does the woodpecker peck?

173. Why the kiwi has a long and narrow beak?

174. Why do the tigers have stripes?

175. Why do some water-birds have so long legs?

176. What are guineapigs?

177. What is protective colouration?

178. Why do male birds have bright colours?

179. How does the humming bird manage to stand still in the mid air?

180. Does bee die soon after it stings?

181. Which bird may steal bright things like rings and trinkets?

WOODPECKER

182. Why is the skylark so favourite with poets?

183. Why are the spiders not caught in their own web?

184. What is a hoopoe?

185. Why does the bull charge at a red piece of cloth?

186. Which bird is called the gem among birds?

187. What is a spoonbill?

188. The name of which creature signifies - hundred legs?

189. What is a cygnet?

190. What is a puffin?

191. What is the bird that can fly backwards besides standing still in the mid air?

192. What is the bird that honks?

193. What is a pheasant?

194. Which is the world's largest flying bird?

195. What is so unusual about the flamingo?

196. The name of which animal means 'no-drinking'?

197. Which is the longest and most poisonous snake?

198. Which is the most destructive insect in the world?

199. Which mammal has the shortest lifespan?

200. What form of marine life was used as coins in earlier India?

201. Are wombats marsupials?

202. How does the porcupine attack?

203. Which kind of bat feeds on blood?

204. What is the sea cucumber?

205. What is a crepuscular animal?

206. What is ethology? Who is called the father of this branch of science?

207. What is bioluminescence?

208. What is a lemur?

209. What is the substance called which forms hair, hooves, claws, nails, feathers etc. in vertebrates?

210. What is limnology?

211. Which bird can attain the highest speed?

212. What are Arctic terns famous for?

213. What is sericulture?

214. What is hibernaculum?

215. What is aestivation?

216. Which is the bird clever enough to sneak its own eggs into other birds' nests for hatching?

BATS

217. Which bird is notorious as the pirate of the polar regions?

218. Who is an ornithologist?

219. What is ornithomancy?

220. What precious things are obtained from oyster-shells?

221. Which animal breaks off its own tail to escape from an attacker?

222. What type of animal is the flying fox?

223. What are llamas?

224. What is WWF? When was it formed?

225. What are Red Data Books?

226. Which is the famous national park where the endangered mountain Gorilla are preserved?

227. In which sanctuary are asiatic lions being protected in India?

228. What are the various animals and birds being protected in Indian Kaziranga National Park?

229. Where is Kanha National Park?

230. Who is the famous author, hunter, conservationist and naturalist after whom a National Park in the footfulls of Shivalok Range in U.P. has been named?

231. Which is the nearest bird sanctuary to Delhi?

232. Where are the white tigers found in India?

233. Which is the wildlife park in the US where puma is kept and protected?

234. What is a herbivore?

235. What is natural selection?

236. What is a salt lick?

237. What is the gestation period of the house mouse?

238. What is the gestation period of the lion?

239. What is the gestation period of human being?

240. What is the number of young born to the Indian elephant at a time?

241. What is the number of young born to the orangutan at a time?

242. What is the home of the river otter called?

243. What is the burrow of the rabbit called?

244. What is the nest of the eagle called?

245. What is the nest of the squirrel called?

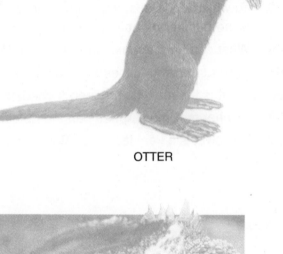

OTTER

246. What is the approximate maximum lifespan of the blue whale?

247. What is the approximate maximum lifespan of the sheep?

248. What is the number of species of sea-snakes?

249. Where are iguanas found?

250. Where is the sunbeam snake found?

251. What is the maximum number of eggs that blue tit lays at a time?

IGUANA

252. How long does the house sparrow live maximum?

253. What is the maximum recorded age of the pheasant?

254. How many eggs does grey heron lay at a time?

255. What is the incubation period of the owl?

256. What is the fledgling period of the king penguin?

257. Which birds come under the family of corvidae?

258. What is the incubation period of the cookoo?

259. Where are toucans found?

260. Where are the larks found?

261. What are the number of species of the swift?

262. What is the duration of pregnancy in the camel?

263. What kind of birds are rheas?

264. What kind of animals are rodents?

265. To which class of animals do sponges belong? What is the number of their species?

TOUCAN

266. What can be the maximum height of the giraffe?

267. At what maximum speed can a golden eagle fly?

268. What is the maximum speed a cheetah can attain?

269. At what maximum speed can the dolphin swim?

270. The swift is a very fast bird. At what maximum speed it can fly?

A NSWERS

1. There are about 30 million different kinds of animals.

2. Only 7-8 per cent of animals are vertebrates.

3. One major difference between animals and plants is that plants do not have senses and motion. Plants can manufacture their own food with the help of light but animals cannot.

4. In most of the cases animals produce their babies by mating.

5. Biology is a branch of science that studies all living things— plants and animals.

6. The two main branches of Biology are Botany and Zoology.

7. Gregor Mendel discovered the Laws of Genetics in 1860.

GREGOR MENDEL

8. The genes we inherit determine and control our character and traits.

9. Evolution is the process of gradual change in the characteristics of living things over many generations.

10. Many millions years ago life emerged from a minute mass of protoplasm, the simplest thing.

11. Charles Darwin, an English naturalist, propounded the Theory of Evolution.

12. The Theory of Evolution is based on the study of fossil remains, present distribution of animals, the study of embryology etc.

13. The Theory of Evolution in brief says that all species have evolved from common ancestors.

CHARLES DARWIN

14. There are about 4,000 kinds of mammals.

15. The mammary glands in the females produce milk for their babies.

16. Fur or hair on the body of mammals insulate them.

17. Mammals are placental because their young ones develop into their mother's womb where they are connected with the umbilical cord called placenta for nourishment.

18. The other organs which the mammals have in common are a large brain, a spinal cord, an extensive nervous system, a heart that pumps blood to all parts of the body.

19. The time between mating or conception and birth of a baby is called gestation?

20. Primates are a class of higher order of mammals. Many types of apes, monkeys and human beings belong to the class called primates.

21. The gorilla is the largest of the primates.

22. Lions are now found only in some parts of Africa and India.

23. A group of lions is known as a 'pride'.

24. The cheetah is the fastest land animal and can run at the speed of 100 km per hour over a short distance.

GORILLA

25. The big cats have stripes or spots on their skin because they help them to camouflage.

26. William Blake.

27. Marsupial mammals mean animals with a pocket or a pouch.

28. A newborn baby kangaroo is hardly an inch in size.

29. A kangaroo can jump upto 3-4 metres at a time.

30. The tree-dwelling small opossum mammals are found in America.

31. The mammals which live in sea are whales, seals, walruses, dolphins and porpoises.

KANGAROO

32. Whales are the largest animals and some of them can be as long as 30 metres.

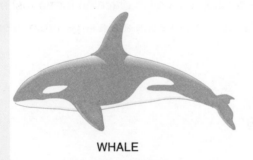

WHALE

DOLPHINS

33. Dolphins are believed to have an elaborate language. They talk in clicking sounds.

34. Blubber is a thick layer of fat which keeps sea mammals warm in the cold water.

35. Seals, sea-lions and walruses are amphibians. They can live both in water and on land.

36. Walrus is the only sea mammal to have a pair of tusks and also a thick moustache.

37. The elephant is the living descendant of the huge and giant animals that roamed all over the earth long long ago.

38. A mammoth was a huge woolly elephant that lived some 12,000 years ago.

39. An elephant can be as tall as 4 metres.

40. The trunk is the most remarkable organ of the elephant. It is its extended nose and upper lip.

41. The elephant's tusks have been the main source of their undoing. They have been killed in thousands for their ivory.

42. There might be some 5,000,000 elephants left now all over the world.

43. At the end of the trunk of an elephant is a little raised point. It is called its 'finger.' It is very useful. With it he can pick up even a needle. The African elephant has two fingers but its Asian relative has only one finger.

44. An Asian elephant can live up to the age of 70 years.

45. There are some 280 different kinds of birds of prey which include eagles, hawks, kites, falcons, vultures, owls, kestrels and harriors.

THE LAMMERGEIER (BEARDED VULTURE)

46. The sparrow hawk skims, dodges and glides low over hedges and copes and then suddenly swoops on an unsuspected victim.

47. Birds are light weight because of hollow bones and very light feathers and wings. Therefore they can fly in the air for a very long duration.

48. Birds have evolved from reptiles. During this evolution their scales got transformed into wings and feathers.

49. Moulting means shedding of feathers. Birds shed their feathers and grow new ones. They shed their feathers few at a time which are soon replaced by new ones.

50. Birds have no teeth and yet there is no problem in digestion of their food. Inside the body of birds there is a muscular bag which grinds the food into digestible particles. This bag is called gizzard. Some birds swallow small stones, and grit to help the grinding process.

51. Protective colouration means matching of colours of the birds to their surroundings and environment. It serves the purpose of camouflage. This resemblance of birds in colour to their habitat and environment tends to make them inconspicuous and protected.

52. The ostrich is the largest living flightless bird. It is found in Africa. Its wings are rudimentary and non-functional.

53. Kiwis are found in New Zealand. It is the smallest flighless bird.

54. Antartica is the favourite haunt of penguins. They are also found in southern Australia, southern Brazil, south-west Africa and New Zealand.

55. The wings of penguins changed into flippers because of long and continuous disuse. They did not use their wings for many many generations and so ultimately forgot how to fly.

OSTRICH

56. There are some 17 species of penguins. The biggest of them is the emperor penguin, over 1 mt in height and 36 kg in weight.

57. Owls feed on mice, moles, insects, lizards, chickens and other domestic fowls.

58. The eyes of owls are very keen and flexible. They can expand and contract as the need be. The owl can open its pupils of the eye wide enough to absorb all the light that might be available at night. Therefore, it can see clearly in the darkness.

PENGUINS

59. The owl has very soft and flexible wings. They enable him to swoop down stealthily and silently on its prey.

60. Yes, the owl can hear very well. Its sense of hearing is very sharp. This helps it a great deal in locating its prey and victims.

61. The owl kills its prey with its sharp talons and beaks and then swallows it whole. Later it vomits out the indigestible parts.

62. The bat is the only mammal that can fly.

63. The two major classes of bats are fruit eating and insect eating bats.

64. Bats find their path and prey by means of echolocation in darkness of night. Bats give out high pitched sounds inaudible to the human ear. These sounds return back to them in the form of echoes and tell them about the obstacles that might be there in their way.

65. Vampires are the only bats that feed on the blood of cattle, dogs, horses, chickens, etc.

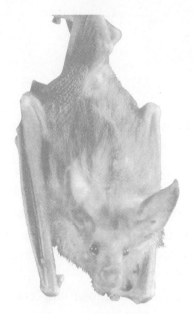

BATS HANG UPSIDE DOWN

VAMPIRE

66. Bats do not and cannot sit on trees. Neither can they stand on their feet. They hang upside down on the high branches of trees.

67. Movement and travel of a large group of birds from one place to another is known as migration.

68. Birds migrate in winters from severe cold regions of the north to warmer regions. They do so because in harsh winters they may not survive nor is there enough food to feed on. In summers they migrate back to their original home. For breeding also they need warm and comfortable climate.

69. The Arctic tern completes a journey of about 22,000 miles every year back and forth.

70. There are a couple of theories about how birds find their way and reach the place of migration. One theory suggests that landmarks during the day and positions of the stars at night guide them in their journey. Another theory suggests that the magnetic field of the earth guides them. But none of these theories are proven.

71. There are over 2,000 different kinds of snakes.

72. The regal python is the largest snake which may measure from 2 to 6 mt in length.

73. The python kills its victims by constriction, that is by squeezing them until they are suffocated.

74. Besides python, boa constrictors and anaconda are large snakes. The former is found in South and Central America and Southern Mexico. The latter is found in India, Malaysia and South America. The African python is also a large snake.

PYTHON

75. The king cobra is the deadliest snake.

76. The king cobra can dilate its neck behind its head to resemble a hood.

77. Rattlesnake is a poisonous American snake which has a bony rattling tail.

78. The rattlesnake's tail is made up of cup-shaped hard, horny joints. They fit loosely into each other. When the snake is disturbed, angry or excited then its tail begins to rattle as a result of the joint striking one another.

79. Snake hatchings break through the egg shell using their egg-tooth.

80. The rattlesnake does not lay eggs but gives birth to live babies.

81. All reptiles that are carnivorous and hunt and feed in water are called crocodilians.

82. Crocodilians include crocodiles, alligators, caymans and gharials. They are found in warm fresh waters and marshes of Africa, Asia, Australia and America.

83. Having caught an animal or bird, they drag it into the water and drown it immediately with a hard blow of their mighty tail.

84. Alligators and crocodiles look alike. But one great difference is that in the case of a crocodile, the fourth tooth of the lower jaw is clearly visible even when its mouth is closed.

GHARIAL

85. One major function of colouring in animals is camouflaging. It helps animals in becoming one with their surroundings.

86. Arborial lizards are those lizards which are associated with trees.

87. The chameleon has transparent skin. Under this skin are layers of cells which have yellow, black and red pigments. When excited, disturbed or angry, its colour cells contract and expand and there is a change of colours.

88. Excitement results in yellow colouring and spots in a chameleon.

89. Tortoises and turtles need not run, because whenever there is any

CHAMELEON

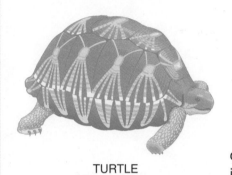

TURTLE

danger, they can retract their head and limbs inside the hard shell which acts as a perfect armour.

90. Turtles and tortoises shoot out their sticky tongues to catch insects to feed on. They can also feed on plants.

91. There are about 3,700 different kinds of lizards.

92. Yes, lizards hibernate in winter.

93. Flying dragon is the flying lizard. It has skiny wings which help it to glide from one branch of a tree to another. It is arborial animal. It actually glides but does not fly.

94. The horned lizards feed on ants.

95. Some 700 million years ago jelly-fish and sponges evolved.

96. About 220 million years ago the age of dinosaurs began.

97. About 65 million years ago dinosaurs became extinct.

98. Birds are supposed to have evolved from a common ancestor called—the Archeopteryx.

99. The extinction of dinosaurs prove the theory of evolution, natural selection and struggle for survival.

100. Cartilaginous animals are those that have their skeletons made of the rubbery substance called cartilage. Sharks and rays are cartilaginous animals.

Chapter 5

101. The largest shark can grow upto 15 mt in length.

102. Some of the sharks like white shark etc. are dangerous because they attack human beings. They have many rows of razor sharp teeth and powerful jaws that can bite through anything.

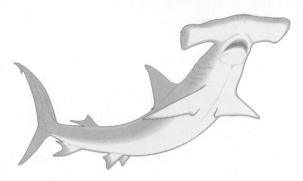

HAMMER SHARK

103. Sharks are long and thin, while rays are flat and broad and have a sting in their tail.

104. Some sharks follow a ship in the hope of picking some food from the ship. Such sharks are called scavenger sharks.

105. Fish absorb oxygen in water through their respiratory organs called gills.

106. Yes, the fish can hear, smell and taste. They have internal ears.

WHALE SHARK

107. There are a few fish that can live out of water for some time. The flying fish can glide over the surface of water through the air for over 400 mt and rise high upto 6 mt above sea water. African cat fish can breathe air through its lungs and live out of water for many days. Tree-climbing fish can also live out of water.

108. Sometimes when water is polluted, fish come out on the surface of water and try to breathe in air.

109. The whale is the largest living animal but it is not a fish but a mammal.

110. Their fins, slim streamlined body with a lot of flexibility and long, forked tail help fishes to be perfect swimmers.

111. The colouring of the fish helps them to match with their background so as not be detected by their predators. They can also change colours to camouflage and blend with their surroundings.

112. Majority of the fish belong to the bony category. Fishes of this category have a bony skeleton and are covered with bony scales.

TIGER BARB—
A COLOURFUL FISH

113. The organs of smell in the fish are located inside their nostrils on the head.

114. Frogs are amphibians and can live on land and in water. When in the tadpole stage they live in water and breathe with their gills. Adult frogs develop lungs and so breathe with them on the land and while in water. They can also breathe through their skin.

115. Yes, frogs can live without breathing for a long time. During winter they often bury themselves under mud and stop breathing. Whatever little oxygen they need, they get from water or moisture through their skins.

116. The popular superstition about salamanders is that they cannot be harmed by fire. But it is not true.

117. Newts are amphibians and look like lizards. They begin their life in water like tadpoles and when adult live on land. The "breeding dress" of the great-crested newt are crests which help him to attract female newts during the breeding season.

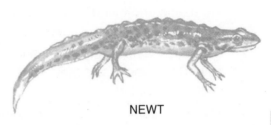

NEWT

118. The female frog lays eggs and they may number from two thousand to eight thousand eggs.

119. Tadpoles have tails but they are absorbed later when their gills are replaced by lungs and other bodily changes take place.

120. A frog takes from 11 to 12 weeks to develop into an adult frog from an egg through a tadpole.

121. A frog or a toad can live up to 30 to 40 years.

122. It is not easy to distinguish a frog from a toad because they have many striking similarities. However, in some respects they differ from each other. Toads lay fewer eggs. They spend most of their adult life on land. Their feet are not webbed and they move by walking or hopping. Frogs lay a large number of eggs. Their skin is relatively thinner. They can jump better than toads.

123. Yes, some of frogs can live on trees. They live there and never come to water even for breeding. They have long fingers and toes which help them to fasten themselves to twigs and branches and also in jumping from one branch to another.

124. The word "amphibian" means "living double life". Frogs, toads, newts and salamanders are amphibian animals that live both in water and on land.

125. There are about 1,000 different species of amphibians.

126. The strange thing about midwife male toad is that it carries the string of eggs around its hind legs till they are hatched.

127. An Australian male frog called the Darwinian frog gulps in the eggs and keeps them safely in a sack under its throat. When they hatch they come out of his mouth.

128. The Brazilian female frog lays its eggs in a nest of mud. They can be found in clusters joined together with a sticky substance.

129. A virus is an ultra-microscopic pathogenic particle. Viruses are totally parasitic and cannot multiply outside a host. They cause diseases among animals and plants and are therefore always harmful.

130. Viruses enter the host and then take over the chemical energy of the cells of the host and multiply rapidly and ultimately destroy the cells. They also cause cells to become malignant.

131. Bacteria are unicellular microbes. Some of them carry diseases but some others are useful and friendly. Some others are not parasitic and can manufacture their food from sunlight and chemicals.

132. Butterflies wear bright and brilliant colours. They are active during day. Moths have dull colours and they are active during night and at evening. They are attracted by light of a lamp etc.

133. There are some 17,000 known varieties of butterflies.

134. The butterfly passes through many changes to become an adult from an egg. It is called metamorphosis. First there are eggs which change into caterpillars. Caterpillars develop into cocoons. Inside the cocoons there is constant change. Finally, the cocoons split open and the young butterfly comes out.

135. Yes, butterflies and moths can smell. Their smelling organs are on their antennae.

136. Ladybirds are friends of farmers because they are very good natural pest-controllers. They feed on aphids, coccids, mites, etc. which are harmful to crops, plants and vegetables.

137. Bacteria were discovered by Antonvan Leeuwen Hoek, a Dutch microscopist and naturalist, in 1683.

LADYBIRD

138. Bacteria are microscopic unicellular germs. They reproduce by binary fission. It means a division of cell into two. It is asexual production of an organism forming into similar but smaller individuals.

139. Bacteria are put into four groups or categories according to their shapes. They are bacilli (rod shaped), cocci (spherical), commas (twisted), and spirilli (spirals).

140. Infection is a disease or disorder not resulting from physical injury but from bacteria.

141. Malaria is caused by the introduction in the human body of a class of single-celled bacteria and parasites. Mosquitoes called Anopheles (females only) mosquito do it while feeding and sucking blood from an infected human being. The bacteria pass to the liver and grow and multiply there very fast. Then they re-enter human blood stream and attack and destroy the red blood cells.

142. There are some 2,000 different kinds of bacteria.

143. Some of the micro-organisms called bacteria are harmless and helpful. They help in the digestion process of men and animals. They are found in intestines where they break the food eaten into small particles which are easily digestible. They also produce certain vitamins.

144. Some bacteria play an important role in nitrogen-fixation. They absorb nitrogen and combine it with oxygen to form nitrates which are then absorbed by plants. Plants are eaten by animals and men to get nitrogen. Bacteria also produce nitrates from dead and decaying animals and plants. They also release nitrogen back in this process. Nitrogen is an essential element for living organisms, forming an essential part of proteins and nucleic acids.

145. Chitin is a substance of which the very tough shell, covering the body of insects is made of. The cover is called exoskeleton.

146. Moulting is shedding of the old skeleton. An insect moults many times in its life-span. Every time an insect moults its old skeleton, it is replaced by a new and bigger one.

147. An insect's eyes are wonderful in the sense that they are not simple but compound. In each of the two eyes there are several lenses. In the eyes of an ant there may be six lenses each but in dragonflies the number of lenses in each eye grows to 30,000 lenses. The larger number of lenses make them see better and perfectly. They can see movement from any direction.

148. There are some 1 million different known and recognised species of insects.

149. Insects feel, hear and smell with the help of their antennae They have their feelers or sensory organs. They are often jointed, mobile and found in pairs on their heads. The antennae have very thin and sensitive hairs on them. They are sensitive even to the slightest air current. Ants, bees, wasps use them for tasting things.

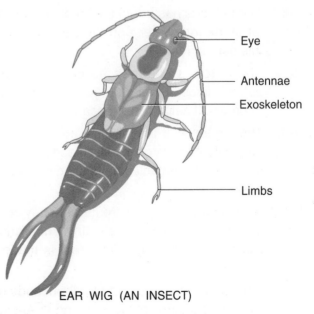

Eye

Antennae

Exoskeleton

Limbs

EAR WIG (AN INSECT)

150. In a hive there are three types of bees—the queen bee, drones and workers.

151. The queen bee's job among honey bees is to lay eggs and not to do anything else.

152. The fertilized eggs in a honey comb develop into either queens or workers (female). There can be only one queen in a hive. The first new queen that comes out of a fertilized egg kills all of her sister queens in their cells and thus becomes the only queen and mother in a hive.

HONEY BEE

153. The job of worker bees is to collect pollen and nectar and produce honey and wax. They also help in cross-pollination of crops and plants.

154. The webs of spiders are made of strong silken threads. These threads are not only sticky but also very strong.

155. Yes, spiders eat up their own web to save protein.

156. An amoeba is a primitive unicellular protozoa. It has no mouth, lungs, gills or legs. And yet it performs all the functions of an organism. It reproduces by binary fission. First its nucleus divides itself into two parts and then the amoeba itself divides into two parts and thus two individual amoebae are born.

157. The octopus got its name because it has eight arms or tentacles, with suckers with which it catches its prey.

158. The octopus has a funnel-siphon with which it shoots out a jet of ink into water and then escapes under the cover of this dark screen.

159. The octopus changes its colours to match that of its surroundings. It can change red to grey, sea-green, yellow or brown. It helps him to escape its enemies by camouflage.

160. The tentacles of the jellyfish are useful in two ways. Firstly they help it to protect itself. Secondly it catches its prey with them. These tentacles have stinging cells that kill the victim easily.

161. Polyps are tiny marine creatures. They are skeleton-forming anemones. They secrete tiny substances of which the skeleton is made up. Coral reef is made up of millions of skeletons of dead polyps.

JELLY FISH

162. The coral reef can spread for thousands of miles. For example, the Great Barrier Reef off the coast of Queensland in Australia is about 2000 km long.

163. A coral atoll is a ring of corals around the edge of an old volcano. When the volcano sinks or the level of seawater rises, the coral grows up and then a coral atoll is left behind the surface. Thus, an atoll is an island in an open ocean made up of coral reefs around a lagoon.

164. Along with other sea-animals with ten legs, the lobster is called a decapod. Deca means ten and pod means feet.

165. A female lobster can lay eggs ranging from 5,000 to 100,000.

166. In the first year of its existence the lobster sheds its hard and horny shell 17 times. This is called moulting. But when it becomes a full adult, moulting is limited to once a year.

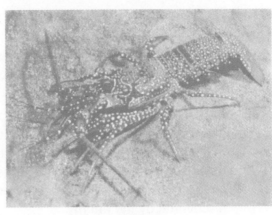

LOBSTER

167. It is kind of hyena which does not actually laugh but makes strange howls while on prowl or when excited.

168. Yes, fishes do smell. Smell helps them to find their way. As the water flows in and out of their nostrils, it activates their sense of smell and they detect a smell.

169. Those fishes which give birth to living babies are called viviparous. And those who lay eggs are called oviparous. Most of the fishes lay eggs.

170. No, fishes do not weep or shed tears. They do not have tear-glands. Tears clean and keep moist our eyes. This function is done in regard to the fishes by the water they live in.

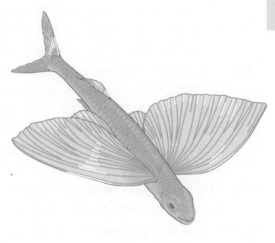

FLYING FISH

171. The snake swings its body side-ways into curves or loops to get speed and easy momentum.

172. The woodpecker can be often seen pecking on the trees. It undertakes this exercise to find out insects and grubs on which it feeds.

173. The kiwi has a long and narrow beak because it helps the bird to search out insects, worms and caterpillars from under the soil and the thick carpet of dead leaves.

174. Tigers have black and yellow stripes because these help them in camouflage. These vertical stripes enable them to hide in the grass, bushes, bamboos etc.

175. Some water-birds like cranes, flamingos, herons etc. have very long legs. The long legs help them to wade about in the shallow and marshy water, finding out small fish on which they subsist.

176. Guinea pigs are not pigs. They are rodents. They are often kept as pets.

177. Birds have colours which help them in camouflage. This protection, so that they may not be detected easily, is known protective colouration.

178. Male birds have bright and brilliant colours so that they may attract their female partners during the mating season. Female birds have dull colours because they have to hatch the eggs and bring up young ones. Dull colours help them from being discovered by the enemy.

FLAMINGO

179. The humming-bird can be seen standing quite still for sometime in the air while sucking the nectar of a flower. It can manage in doing so by beating its wings very fast. On a average the humming bird can beat its wings about 55 times a second. Really a wonderful feat.

180. The belief that a bee dies soon after it stings is not based on facts. A bee can use its sting many times over. However the sting remains sticking into the skin of the person.

HUMMING BIRD

181. The magpie is a familiar bird. It is fond of bright things like jackdaw and other members of this family. It will steal rings, pins and trinkets.

182. The skylark has been a popular bird in poetry because of its ecstatic song. As it hovers in the sky, it poures forth its musical notes which are often trilling and liquid.

183. The web is so sticky that it can catch the spider too. But because a spider is in its own nest and home, he knows the safe passage and some of the threads that would really not stick to it. A spider is an expert both in weaving and recognising the sticky and non-sticky silken threads of its webs.

184. The hoopoe is a very striking bird with its cinnamon-pink plumage which is barred across the wings. It has a large barred crest and a long, thin and slightly curved bill. In its flight it looks like a big butterfly.

185. Bullfighting is a popular sport in Spain. There is a belief that red colour makes a bull angry and causes him to charge. But the fact is that the bull is colour blind. What makes the bull charge at the red cloth is not its colour but its waving by the matodor. A cloth of any other colour will do as well.

186. The kingfisher is called the gem among birds because of its bright and dazzling colours. In its flight, during clear and sunny day, it appears like a streak of blue light.

187. What is so remarkable about the spoonbill is its long spatulate beak. It can be often seen feeding in soft mud and water at the edges of lakes, ponds and marshes. Its plumage is white like that of a heron.

188. The centipede is a creature which signifies hundred legs.

189. The young one of a swan is called a cygnet.

190. The puffin is a remarkable bird with its massive and striped bill. The stripes are grey-blue, scarlet and yellow. It stands in an upright pose. Sometimes it may be found in large numbers. It feeds on small fish for which it dives and swims under the water.

PUFFIN BIRD

191. It is the humming bird which can fly backwards and remain stand still for quite sometime in the air by beating its wings very, very fast on an average 50 times in a second.

192. It is the goose that honks. The geese are of many different types and belong to the family of ducks and swans. A goose may be wild or domestic.

193. The pheasant is very attractive and beautiful bird with its so colourful plumage. It has long chestnut brown tail with blackbars. Its chestnut brown plumage are handsomely marked with black and cream colours.

194. The large American vulture called condor is the largest flying bird. Its wingspan is of about 3 metres. It is a carrion feeder. It has naked head and neck, powerful and sharp hooked beak and blackish plumage. It can spot a carcass from a very long distance because of its excellent eyesight.

AMERICAN ANDEAN CONDOR

195. What makes the flamingo so striking are its large size, long, broad beak bent at the middle, very long and slender neck, long, thin leg and pinkish - rosy plumage. It is a tropical wading water - bird found in large colonies in shallow lakes and lagoons.

FLAMINGO

196. Koala means 'no drink' because it seldom drinks

KOALA

any water. It is the largest tree-dwelling marsupial mammal. It is found in Australia and has beak-like snout, tufted ears and no tail. It looks like a teddy-bear. It comes out at night to feed on the leaves of eucatyptus. Its babies are 25mm long weighing just five grams each. They remain in their mother's pouch for about six months.

197. The king cobra is the longest and most poisonous snake. It is about 2 metres long and capable of dialating its neck to form a large hood behind its head. The king cobra is found in India and Africa and feed upon rodents. They are good friends of farmers as they destroy rodents.

198. The locust is the most destructive insect in the world. They have short and well developed ovipositor which is used for excavating hole in the ground for laying eggs. There are nine species of the locust in the world of which 3 are common in India.

199. The shrew has the shortest lifespan among the mammals. It is a mouselike mammal that feeds on insects. It is characterized by a small body, little eyes, sharp pointed snout, small ears and a long tail.

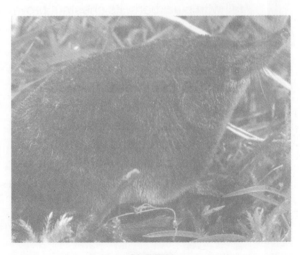

200. Cowry-shells were used as small coins in India in early times. Cowries are small gastropods with very smooth shell, oval and rounded on top. They are flat beneath and have long narrow

SHREW

opening. On both sides of them there are toothers and channels at each end. They are found crawling among coral reefs. Now they are chiefly used for decoration and ornaments among tribals and primitive people.

WOMBAT

201. The marsupials are the mammals which give birth to immature babies. These are then nursed by their mothers inside their pouch or marsupiam. Marsupiam is a kind of pocket on the side of abdomen of the females. Yes, wombat is a marsupial. It is herbivorous, about 1.25 mt long with short legs and strong claws and rudimentary tail. It is found in Australia and neighbouring Tasmania.

202. The porcupine has sharp and long quills or spines all over its body. The porcupine rushes backwards to attack the enemy with its quills. It is a burrowing animal and has powerful claws for digging burrows.

203. The vampire bat has razor sharp teeth for cutting and feeding on blood-diet. It is a small bat, less than 10 cm long and found in south and Central America.

204. The sea-cucumber is a sausage shaped spineless marine creature. Its mouth is surrounded by hollow branching tentacles which may be 10-30 in numbers. It feeds on plankton. Sea-cucumbers are edible and are used as food in many countries.

205. The crepuscular animals are active in twilight when day and night meet. They hunt and become active during pre-dawn and dusk. The nocturnal animals are active during night and diurnal animals at daytime. Thus, all the animals can be put under these three broad catagories.

206. Ethology is a branch of biology, which studies animal behaviour in relation to its environment and habitat. The Australian biologist and Nobel laureate Konard Lorenz is called as father of ethology.

207. The production of light by living creatures is known as bioluminescence. Glow-worms and fireflies are good examples of these creatures. They produce light by oxiding luciferm in the presence of an enzyme. Many marine organisms also emit light.

208. A lemur is a primate and nocturnal animal. It is 20 to 100 cm long with pointed muzzle and long bushy tail. It is related to monkeys and lives in forests. When it runs, it keeps its tail and back erect. Lemurs are found in Madagascar only.

209. The substance that forms hair, hooves, claws, nails, feathers, horns etc. is known as keratin. It is a nitrogenous substance and a kind of protein.

210. The scientific study of freshwaters like lakes, ponds, rivers, streams etc. and the animals and plants living in them is known as limnology.

211. The peregrine falcon is the fastest bird in the world. This so powerful bird has no match in speed and skill in flight. It can overtake any other bird in speed. It feeds on sea-birds, pigeons, waders and others both big and small. It is found at sea-coasts, moutains and cliffs.

212. The Arctic tern is the bird that migrates the longest distance. It belongs to a group of sea-birds: Aves. It has narrow beak, short red legs, narrow and tapered wings. Its tail is forked and 25-40 cm long. It is of grey colour with black crown and nape. They make their terneries on rocky islands and on sandy seashores.

213. Sericulture involves the breeding of silk worms for the production of silk.

214. The winter shelter for animals and plants is called hibernaculum. A bulb or a bud by which a plant survives severe winter is a hibernaculum. Many animals like bear etc. hibernate and sleep in their winter shelters when it is too cold to live and there is hardly any food to eat.

215. Dormancy and sleep during hot and dry season by animals is called aestivation.

216. The cuckoo is really clever enough to sneak its own eggs into the nests of others for hatching. Thus, it is a parasite who does not care for its young ones. Yet it is a very popular bird liked for its sweet notes. It feeds on all kinds of insects and caterpillars. Its coming heralds the advent of the spring season followed by summer.

217. The skua is nick-named as the pirate of the polar regions because it steals the eggs of other sea-birds and also fish from them. It does not hesitate in chasing other birds even larger than itself. It feeds on fishes snatched from other birds, eggs, nestlings, smaller birds and carrion.

218. Ornithology is a branch of zoology that undertakes study of birds. A person having a sound knowledge of this subject is called ornithologist.

219. People have been trying to know and foretell the future or the unknown by various means. Ornithomancy is one of them. Under it people practice divination with the help of birds. They observe their flights and other behaviour to have a peep in the future.

220. Pearls are obtained from the shells of some oysters and molluscs. Young oysters are mostly males but half of them later turn into females. Some of them change their sex every year. They are used as food by men and so cultivated and raised in oyster-beds.

221. The lizard would often break off its own tail to escape attack and death. It is a reptile quadruped having moving eyelids, ear drums and a long tail. Lizards are of many kinds.

222. The flyingfox is a large Asiatic fruit-eating bat. It is a nocturnal mammal whose forelimbs are formed as wings. A flap of skin is stretched between all four digits, legs and the tail. It is a voracious eater and can be seen during the day in large number hanging down from the branches of a tree.

223. The llama is a domesticated or wild guanaco. It has a reddish brown body and found in South America. They live in small herds in which there are many females, an adult male and many young ones. It is like a camel but much smaller and without a hump.

LLAMA

224. WWF stands for the World Wildlife Fund international. It was formed in 1961 and has its head quarters at Morges in Switzerland. Its chief aim and object is to collect funds and distribute it for wildlife conservation throughout the world.

225. Red Data Books are directories that provide uptodate information about the animal species which are on the verge of extinction or are rare.

226. In Albert National Park, Congo, Africa, the Mountain Gorilla is protected and preserved.

227. Asiatic lions are being protected at Gir National Park, Gujarat.

228. Rhinoes, leopards, gibbons, pythons, wild bears, tigers, pelicans, storks, floricans, swamp deer, elephants, wild buffaloes are being conserved in Kaziranga National Park.

229. Kanha National Park is in Madhya Pradesh.

230. This National Park has been named after the famous man Jim Corbett. It is called Jim Corbet National Park.

231. Ghana Bird Sanctuary, Keoladeo National Park, Bharatpur in Rajasthan is the nearest bird sanctuary to Delhi.

232. White tigers in India are found in Rewa, Madhya Pradesh.

233. The puma is being kept and protected in Everglades National Park, Florida, USA.

PUMA

234. A herbivore is an animal which subsists on plants and vegetables.

235. Natural selection is a theory of evolution of organisms propounded by Charls Darwin. According to this theory nature allows the survival and growth of those species which are best adapted to conditions of their environment and habitat.

236. Salt lick is a place where animals come to lick natural salt-deposit at the surface.

237. The gestation period of the house mouse is 20 days.

238. The gestation period of the lion is 105-108 days.

239. The gestation period of the human being is 267 days.
240. The number of the young born to the Indian elephant at a time is one.
241. The number of the young born to the orangutan at a time is one.
242. The home of the river otter is called hott.
243. The burrow of the rabbit is called warren.
244. The nest of the eagle is called eyrie.
245. The nest of the squirrel is called drey.
246. The approximate maximum lifespan of the blue whale is 90 years.

ORANGUTAN

247. The approximate maximum lifespan of the sheep is 22 years.
248. The number of species of seasnake is 50.
249. Iguanas are found in north and south America, West Indies, Galapagos, Fiji and Madagascar.
250. Sunbeam snake is found in India.
251. The blue tit lays maximum 12-14 eggs at a time.
252. The house sparrow lives maximum for 8 year.
253. The maximum recorded age of the pheasant is 8 years.
254. The grey heron lays 4-5 eggs at a time.
255. The incubation period of the owl is 30 days.
256. The fledgling period of the king penguin is 360 days.
257. Crows, magpies and jays come under the family of corvidae.
258. The incubation period of the cuckoo is 12 days.
259. Toucans are found in South America.
260. Larks are found on all the continents.
261. The number of the species of the swift is about 80.
262. The duration of pregnancy in the camel is 406 days.
263. The rheas are flightless, swift in running, ground-nestling birds. They feed on vegetation and insects, like ortrich they have short wings and no tailfeathers.
264. Beavers, squirrils, nice, timings etc. are rodents. They have a pair of upper and lower inciros that grow throughout their life. They are generally herbivorous . They grow and have closed digits?
265. Sponges belong to the family of porifera. The number of their species is 10,000.
266. The maximum height of the giraffe can be 5.5 mt.
267. The golden eagle can fly at the maximum speed of 300 km or 185 miles per hour.
268. The cheetah can attain a maximum speed of 110 km or 68 miles per hour.
269. The dolphin can swim at the maximum speed of 64 km or 40 miles per hour.
270. The swift can fly at the maximum speed of 200 km or 120 miles per hour.

ENVIRONMENT

Chapter 6

ENVIRONMENT

 UESTIONS

1. What is environment?

2. Why is Earth the only known living planet?

3. What has caused a big hole in the ozone layer?

4. What is the work of the ozone layer?

5. What is atmosphere?

6. What is the percentage of nitrogen in the atmosphere?

7. Why is there no atmosphere on the Moon?

8. Upto what height does the atmosphere extend from the surface of the Earth?

9. Air has weight and pressure but why do we not feel it?

10. What is exosphere? What does it consist of?

11. What is biosphere?

12. What is ecology?

13. What is symbiotic relationship ?

14. How many different species are there in the biosphere?

15. Why does smoke occur ?

16. What is noise?

17. What is the level of the sound in a quiet conversation?

18. Why does the quality of life deteriorate?

Poisonous wastes, such as oil into rivers, lakes and seas

Untreated sewage in seas and rivers

Waste gases from factories and vehicles

SOURCES OF POLLUTION

19. Which are the main polluting substances?

20. Which are some of the diseases caused by pollution?

21. What is a food chain?

22. What is the harmful result of destruction of forests and wildlife?

23. What is conservation?

24. What contaminates our various sources of water?

25. What is meant by renewable resources of energy?

26. What is radiation?

27. Why can we see radiation of light?

28. What is responsible for all recycling processes?

29. What is radioactive radiation?

30. Which colour has the longest wavelength?

31. What is ozone?

32. How is ozone formed in the atmosphere?

33. How does the ozone layer protect us?

34. How is ozone useful to us?

35. What are wavelength and frequency?

36. Why is nitrogen essential?

37. Which bacteria help in nitrogen fixation?

38. What are the two classes of denitrifying bacteria?

39. What will be the world population by the year 2025?

40. Who is mainly responsible for air, water and soil pollution?

41. What is the rate of growth of human population per year?

42. Why people in cities are living in very inhuman conditions?

43. What is 'green house effect'?

44. Which gas works like a green house glass? What is its result?

45. At what rate has the temperature of the Earth's oceans increased in the recent past?

46. To what new and prolonged health hazards does global warming expose human beings?

47. What is the result of a nuclear explosion?

48. What does stratospheric fallout mean?

49. How do radioactive particles get into the human and animal body? What is its effect?

50. What does 'extinct species' mean?

51. Why have most of the animal species vanished from the Earth?

BISON (EXTINCT)

52. Where was the Tasmanian wolf found? What did it look like?

53. Which animal, now extinct, was a combination of a zebra and a horse?

54. How much of the natural world has been destroyed during the last 25 years by human activity?

55. What is the main cause of rapid deterioration of environment and decline in biodiversity?

56. Why have dodos become extinct?

57. What does the term 'endangered species' mean?

58. What was average global temperature in 1995 in comparison to 15.38°C in 1990?

59. What is the effect of the rising global temperature?

60. How can environment friendly products be identified?

TASMANIAN WOLF

61. India has been identified as one of the mega-centres of biological diversity. How many animal and plant species have been identified in India?

62. What is fauna?

63. What is fossil fauna?

64. What is flora?

65. In a food chain there are different levels. Which species come to the first or lowest level in the food chain?

LEVEL IV :	Tertiary consumers or Third order consumers. **Carnivores** e.g. foxes and owls.
LEVEL III :	Secondary consumers or Second order consumers. **Carnivores** (flesh eating animals).
LEVEL II :	Primary consumers or First order consumers. (Plant eating animals).
LEVEL I :	Producers : green plants.

FOOD CHAIN

66. When is the World Forestry Day observed?

67. When is Earth Day observed?

68. When is World Environment Day observed? What is its purpose?

69. How the indiscriminate use of pesticides damage our fragile ecology of soils?

70. What is an oil-slick? How is it harmful to our environment?

71. What is a habitat?

72. Hinduism is considered as the religion of nature. In which sacred and ancient book the objects of creature like Agni (fire), Vayu (Air), Indra (rain god), Surya (sun), Soma (moon) etc. have been defied?

73. Many Hindu gods and goddesses have been in very close association with nature. With which tree has Krishna been associated?

74. To which god has basil been so sacred?

75. To which goddess is lotus so dear?

76. Gautma Buddha got enlightenment under a tree. What tree was that?

77. Which tree is closely associated with Shiva?

78. In the arid areas of Rajasthan a particular community is very much committed to the preservation of trees and protection of animals. They would even sacrifice their lives for this causes. Which is this community?

BUDDHA

79. What is ecological ethics?

80. What is environmental determinism?

81. Buddha got enlightenment under the Bodhi tree and then again entered into nirvana under a tree. What was this tree?

82. Who for the first time proposed the term 'Ecosystem'?

83. What is UICN? When was it founded?

84. What is mutualism?

85. What is communalism?

86. Rivers are considered very sacred and worshipworthy. Which river in India is considered most sacred?

87. Which river is regarded as one of the two sisters of Yama, the Lord of Death?

88. Which are the main Himalayan rivers?

89. Besides rivers, animals and birds are also held in respect in India as an integral part of environment. Which animal is associated with Shiva.

90. Which is the mount and vehicle of Vishnu?

91. Peacock is the vehicle of which god?

92. Goddess Durga rides an animal which is as beautiful as fierce. Which is this animal?

93. Who is the daughter of Himalaya, the abode of snow and ice?

94. With which goddess is elephant associated?

95. Even a rise of 0.3° Fahrenheit in global temperature may prove disastrous as is being now experienced. There have been unprecedented droughts, forest fires, floods, hurricanes cyclones, heatwaves, abnormally hot summers etc. What is the cause of this rise in global temperature?

96. In India in 1984 a notable environment disaster took place in which thousands of people died? What was this disaster?

97. The Sunderbans of India and Bangladesh, the largest delta, is now under threat? What is the cause of this threat?

98. In one of the seals belonging to one of the ancient civilizations of India, a woman is shown with a tree growing from her. Which is this civilizaiton? What does it signify?

ANSWERS

1. The combined form of all the physical, chemical and biological factors that surround the Earth and its living beings is its environment.

2. The Earth is the only living planet because its environment protects and sustains life. Such atmosphere does not exist on any other planet known to man.

3. Air pollution has caused a big hole in the ozone layer of the Earth.

4. The ozone layer protects all living beings on the Earth from the harmful effects of the ultraviolet rays.

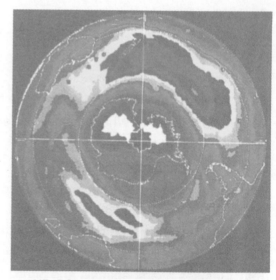

AIR POLLUTION HAS CAUSED A BIG HOLE IN THE OZONE LAYER

5. Atmosphere is the gaseous envelope and mantle that surrounds the Earth.

6. Atmosphere consists of 78% of nitrogen.

7. There is no atmosphere on the Moon because of very poor gravitational pull and force of the moon.

8. The Earth's atmosphere extends upto 50 km from its surface.

9. Air has both weight and pressure but we do not feel it because there is air inside us.

10. The outermost layer of the Earth's atmosphere is called exosphere. It consists mainly of helium and hydrogen.

11. Biosphere is the total area of the Earth's surface that is inhabited by animals and plants.

12. Ecology is the study of the relationship between living beings and their environment. Under this subject interrelationship between living organisms and environment is analysed and studied.

13. In symbiotic relationship there is communalism, mutual benefit and friendship. It means interdependence and natural friendly relationship with the rest of nature and living beings.

14. Biosphere consists of some 35,000 species of living beings including human beings.

15. There is smoke when fuels like oil, wood, coal, etc. are burnt and the combustion is not complete. If the substances could be burnt completely there would be no smoke.

16. A sound becomes noise when it is very loud, disturbing and unmusical. Sound is a physiological sensation received by the ears.

17. In a quiet conversation the level of sound is 20-30 decibels.

18. When there is too much of pollutants in the atmosphere, the balance of nature is disturbed and quality of life deteriorates.

19. Smoke, lead from petrol, untreated sewage, oil-spills, discharged gases, non-degradable insecticides and industrial waste are the main pollutants.

20. Some of the diseases caused by pollution are malaria, dengue, cholera and respiratory diseases.

21. A food chain is a series of organisms through which energy in the form of food is transferred.

22. Destruction of forests and wildlife has resulted in floods, droughts and

AIR POLLUTION

forest fires. The rain patterns have changed and soil erosion is taking place very fast.

23. Conservation means protection of the environment. It also means proper consideration in the use of various Earth resources like water, soil, energy, wildlife, forests, minerals, etc.

24. The toxic chemicals, industrial wastes and untreated sewage, etc. discharged into seas, rivers and lakes contaminate our various water resources.

COMMON SOURCES OF WATER POLLUTION

- MINERAL OILS & HEAVY METALS
- DETERGENTS & FERTILIZERS
- HERBICIDES & PESTICIDES
- ORGANIC WASTES
- SILT HIGH TEMPERATURE
- RADIOACTIVE WASTES
- DOMESTIC SEWAGE
- MINING & INDUSTRIAL WASTES

25. Forests, grasslands, wildlife, soil, wind and the sun are renewable sources of energy.

26. Radiation is emission or sending out of rays, wave motion or particles from a source.

27. We can see or feel light because it is a shortwave radiation.

28. The sunlight is responsible for all re-cycling processes.

RAIN FORESTS OF PERU

29. Radioactive radiation comes from radioactive substances or nuclear fission.

30. Red light or colour has the longest wavelength.

31. Ozone is a form of oxygen which contains 3 atoms of oxygen in a molecule. It is bluish in colour and chemically very active.

32. Ozone is formed in the atmosphere when oxygen in the air is subjected to an electric discharge.

33. The ozone layer is in the upper atmosphere and is responsible for absorbing a large amount of ultraviolet radiation from the Sun. Without this ozone-shield, the Earth would be subjected to many harms including death of many plants and skin cancer to human beings.

NUCLEAR FISSION : A NUCLEUS SPLITS AND EACH PART MAKES ANOTHER NUCLEUS SPLIT

34. Ozone is useful to us in many ways. It kills germs very effectively and quickly and is useful to purify water and other substances such as flour, wax, etc.

35. The distance between waves in radiation is called wavelength. The number of waves passing a given point each second is called the frequency.

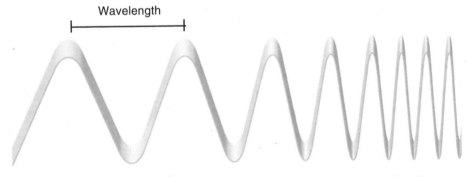

Wavelength

Longer Wavelength, Low Frequency   Shorter Wavelength, High Frequency

36. Nitrogen is essential for all living beings as it forms an essential part of proteins and nucleic acids.

37. The bacteria called dizotrophs help in nitrogen fixation. They consume nitrogen and combine it with oxygen to make nitrates which can be absorbed by plants. Animals absorb nitrogen by eating plants.

38. The two classes of denitrifying bacteria are symbiotic and non-symbiotic.

39. The world population would be 8,500 million by the year 2025.

40. Man is wholly and mainly responsible for air, water and soil pollution.

41. The human population is growing by over 86 million persons every year.

42. People in cities are living in very inhuman conditions because they have turned into the centres of sewage, pollution and garbage.

43. It is the effect produced in a green house covered on all sides by transparent glass. The solar radiation is admitted into the green house and absorbed by plants. The longer wavelength infrared radiation cannot escape through the glass and the inner temperature of the glass house increases considerably.

44. Carbon dioxide works like green house glass and traps much of the Sun's heat and radiation. This has resulted in retention of extra heat by the atmosphere, global warming and increase in the Earth's temperature.

FOREST FIRE

45. It is estimated that global warming is causing a rise in temperature of the Earth's oceans by 1°C per decade.

46. Global warming exposes millions of human beings to new and prolonged health hazards like widespread malaria, dengue and such other dangerous illnesses.

47. A nuclear explosion results in a lot of heat generation and rain of radioactive atoms and particles. Tonnes of radioactive dust is spread and blown off into the atmosphere. This falls to earth as radioactive fallout.

48. Stratospheric fallout means final deposition of radioactive atoms, dust and particles spread over a period of many years.

49. The radioactive particles get into the human and animal body with water, food and air taken in. The radioactive dust falls on plants, fruits and the soil. The soil absorbs it which the plants take in through the roots. Men and animals eat the plants or

their products and then become victims of many diseases as their defence mechanism is weakened considerably.

QUETZEL (EXTINCT ANIMAL)

SNOW LEOPARD (EXTINCT)

50. Extinct species is that whose number has been reduced to nil.

51. They have vanished because of misdeeds of man. In the past several decades the rate of their extinction accelerated because of their killing, hunting, pollution and loss of breeding place and habitat.

52. The Tasmanian wolf was found on the Tasmanian Island, near Australia. It looked like a combination of a wolf, a tiger, a dog and a kangaroo. It had a head like a wolf, a tail like a dog, stripes like a tiger and a pouch like a kangaroo.

53. It was the quagga which looked like a zebra and a horse. It had black stripes like a zebra on its head and shoulders and the rest of its body looked like a horse.

54. One third of the natural world has been destroyed by human activity in the past 25 years, the greatest period of destruction since the extinction of dinosaurs.

QUAGGA

55. The pressure of human consumption has been the main cause of rapid deterioration of environment and decline in biodiversity.

56. Dodos became extinct because of their killing by men for meat in large numbers. They could neither fly nor run and so became an easy prey for men and animals.

57. Endangered species is one that may soon become extinct if not protected and preserved, e.g. Panda.

PANDA (ENDANGERED SPECIES)

DODO

58. The average global temperature in 1995 was 15.39°C in comparison to 15.38°C of 1990.

59. The rising global temperature leads to more intense and violent storms, release of more energy in the atmosphere by the oceans and change in the climate.

60. The products which satisfy the requirements and are up to the standards of Indian environment are environment friendly. They carry the label - ECOMARK.

61. Nearly 81,000 species of animals and 45,000 species of animals have been identified in India.

62. The aggeregtion of animal species characteristic of a certain locality, region or environment is fauna.

63. The animals found fosilized in certain geological formations or accruing in specified time intervals of the past, is referred as fossil fauna.

64. The assemblage of plants of a given geological formation, environment or region is known as flora. It is the plant life of any particular area and or of any particular time.

65. The position each species occupies within a food chain is called a feeding level. Plants come to the first or lowest level of the food chain.

66. March 21 is observed as World Forestry Day.

67. April 22 is observed as Earth Day.

68. World Environment Day is observed on 5th June every year. The purpose of this observation is to spread awareness about protection and conservation of environment among the masses.

69. The indiscriminate use of pesticides seriously damage the fragile ecology of air and soils by weakening the micro-organisms in it.

70. Oil, discharged naturally or by accident or design that float on the surface of water and carried by wind, currents and tides is colled oilslick. Oil slicks and spillages from supertankers cause great harm to various forms of marine life and pollute environment.

71. Habitat is a place where plants and animals naturally grow and live in the natural environment.

72. It is in the Vedas, the most ancient religions text of Hinduism that Agni, Vayu, Indra, Surya, Soma etc. have been defied.

73. Krishna has been closely associated with Kadamba tree. He is often shown under it.

74. Basil has been very sacred with Vishnu.

75. To goddess Lakshmi lotuses have been very dear and sacred.

76. The tree under which Gautam Buddha got enlightenment was the pipal tree, which is now known as the Bodhi Tree.

77. The Vilva tree is closely associated with Shiva.

78. The community in the arid areas of Rajasthan committed so much to the conservation of trees and beasts in Vishnois.

79. Ecological ethics means a change in attitude of mankind towards man, society and nature so as to realize that man is an integral part of nature.

80. Environmental determinism means a belief that all human cultures are deeply influenced and moulded by environment and natural phenomena.

81. The tree under which Buddha entered into nirvana was a Sal tree.

82. The term 'Ecosystem' was first proposed by A.G. Tansley.

83. The full form of UICN is International Union for the Conservation of Nature and the Resources. It was founded in 1948 and has its headquarters at Morges, Switzerland.

84. Mutualism is association between two organisms of different species which is beneficial to both. For example, a bird picking the teeth of a crocodile that has just swallowed a big beast.

85. Communalism is a relationship and interaction between two species or organisms in which one species benefits while the other remains unaffected. For example small animals seeking protection from beasts of prey where elephants are.

86. The Ganges is regarded as the most sacred river in India.

87. The river Yamuna is regarded as one of the two sisters of Yama, the Lord of Death.

88. Ganga, Yamuna, Brahmaputra and Sindhu are the main Himalyan rivers.

89. The Bull Nandi is associated with Shiva.

90. Garuda or eagle is the vehicle and mount of Vishnu.

91. Peacock is the vehicle of Kartikeya

92. It is the lion on which goddess Durga rides.

93. Parvati is the daughter of Himalaya or Himavan.

94. Elephants are associated with the goddess Lakshmi, the goddess of wealth and prosperity.

95. The main cause of the rise in global temperature is indiscriminate burning of fossil fuels world wide. Generation and release of industrial gases that deplete the ozone layer is another cause. They result in disastrous climatic changes and havocs.

96. It was the disaster of Bhopal where Union Carbide's pesticide plant leaked toxic gases and 10,000 people died.

97. The Sunderbans are under threat because of over exploitation of this marine area for fuel, fodder, timber and fishes.

98. The seal depicting a tree growing from the female figure is from the Indus Vally Civilization. It means unity with nature in all respects.

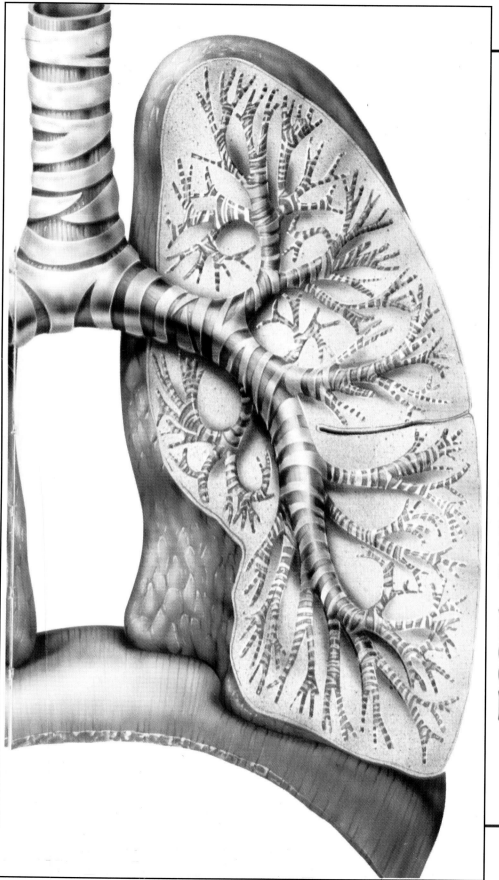

THE HUMAN BODY, HEALTH AND DISEASES

Chapter 7

THE HUMAN BODY, HEALTH & DISEASES

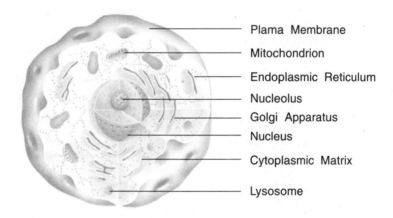

Plama Membrane

Mitochondrion

Endoplasmic Reticulum

Nucleolus

Golgi Apparatus

Nucleus

Cytoplasmic Matrix

Lysosome

STRUCTURE OF A CELL

QUESTIONS

1. What is the practical application of anatomy?

2. Who made the first detailed dissections on animals and made many discoveries about the human body?

3. Who is considered the father of modern human anatomy?

4. The invention of what in the 17th century revolutionised the study of human anatomy and physiology?

5. What is histology?

6. How has Claude Bernard made a significant contribution to the study of human anatomy and physiology?

7. Which disease has now been eradicated and which one has become curable?

8. What functions does the skeleton system perform?

9. What prevents bones from being brittle?

10. What is bone marrow?

11. What holds the bone together at the joints?

12. What are the different kinds of joints found in the human body?

13. Give an example of a ball and socket joint.

14. What is the main function of muscles?

15. What lends power to muscles?

16. How many cells there might be in a medium-sized muscle?

17. Why are many muscles found in pairs?

18. Why is a muscle fatigued?

19. How many muscles are there in all in our body?

20. How much time does a muscle take to contract?

21. What is digestion?

22. What are the various organs that help in the process of digestion?

23. What connects all digestive organs into a chain?

24. What is the stomach and what is its function?

25. What happens to the undigested food?

KNEE JOINT

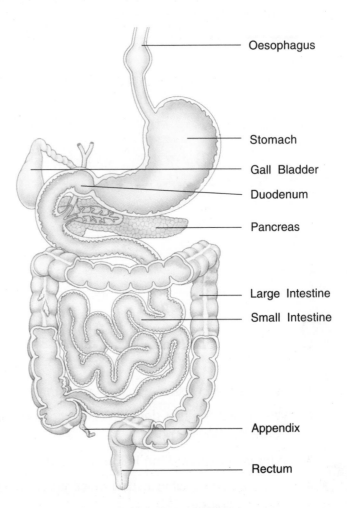

Oesophagus

Stomach

Gall Bladder

Duodenum

Pancreas

Large Intestine

Small Intestine

Appendix

Rectum

DIGESTIVE SYSTEM

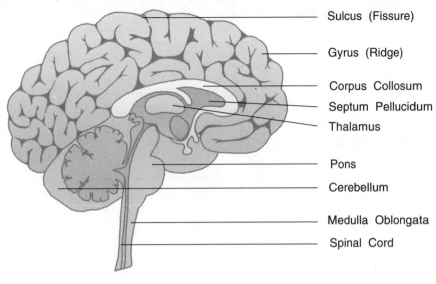

STRUCTURE OF HUMAN BRAIN

26. How does human brain appear?

27. What is the largest part of the human brain called?

28. Which part of our brain is responsible for our conscious behaviour?

29. Which parts of the brain constitute the brain stem?

30. What is the function of the pons?

31. What is breathing?

32. What does our lungs look like?

33. Which organ in our body is responsible for controlling and regulating our breathing?

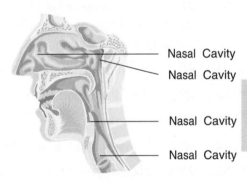

THE RESPIRATORY SYSTEM

34. Of what organs does the respiratory system consist?

35. By what another name is our circulatory system known?

36. What functions does the circulatory system perform?

37. Which are the two circulatory systems?

38. What are the two stages of the heart-beat called?

39. What is the average normal heart beat at rest?

40. How can we hear heart beat?

41. What is the shape of red blood cells?

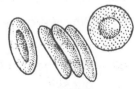

RBC

42. How much blood does the body of an adult human being carry?

43. What does the blood transport?

44. What part do the giant white blood cells play in the body?

45. How many blood cells are there in each cubic millimetre of our blood?

46. What is plasma?

47. Why we need food or energy?

48. What is metabolism?

49. What is a calorie?

50. What is the calorie value of one gram fat and one gram carbohydrate?

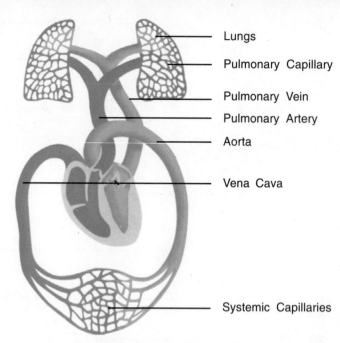

Lungs
Pulmonary Capillary
Pulmonary Vein
Pulmonary Artery
Aorta
Vena Cava
Systemic Capillaries

PULMONARY AND SYSTEMIC CIRCULATION

51. What should be the balanced diet for an average man?

52. Why do children need more calories than grown-up people?

53. What is vitamin?

54. What diseases result in our body for want of vitamins?

55. What deficiency disease is caused by lack of vitamin B1?

56. Why is scurvy caused?

57. Why is vitamin D essential for our body?

58. What is epidermis?

59. Why can stains on our skin be removed so easily?

60. What causes the colour of the skin?

61. Why we do not feel pain when we cut our nails?

62. Which pigment can sunlight produce in our skin?

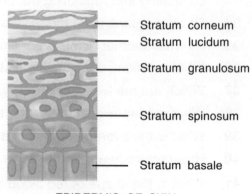

Stratum corneum
Stratum lucidum
Stratum granulosum
Stratum spinosum
Stratum basale

EPIDERMIS OF SKIN

63. What is our eye like?

64. How do we see things?

65. Of how many light-sensitive cells is retina made up? What are these cells called?

66. What are the three kinds of cone cells?

67. What is the function of the nose?

68. What is the number of the smell receptors and where are they located?

69. How do the smell receptors work?

70. Why do some animals have big external ears? How does it help them?

71. How does the process of hearing take place?

72. What are teeth used for?

73. How does a tooth get its nourishment?

74. What is collective dentition?

75. Why should we be very careful in our oral (dental) hygiene?

76. What is DNA?

77. What is the basis of classification of human blood?

78. What are the four blood groups?

79. Who suggested these blood groups for the first time?

80. What is dialysis?

81. What is a sweat-gland? What is the function of sweat-glands?

82. What is a fingerprint?

83. What is a twin?

84. Good health depends on what? Chance or choice?

85. What is puberty?

86. What is adolescence?

87. What is menopause?

88. What is asexual reproduction?

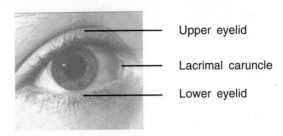

THE HUMAN EYE

Upper eyelid

Lacrimal caruncle

Lower eyelid

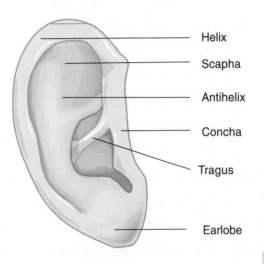

Helix

Scapha

Antihelix

Concha

Tragus

Earlobe

EXTERNAL HUMAN EAR

89. Which is the odd one out?

    (a) Bacteria   (b) Viruses   (c) Fungi   (d) Fruits

90. Which is the odd one out?

    (a) Haemophilia (b) Health   (c) Anaemia   (d) TB

91. Which is the odd one out?

    (a) Beriberi   (b) Rickets   (c) Scurvy   (d) Cold

92. Which is the odd one out?

    (a) Antibody   (b) Immunity   (c) Infection   (d) Antigen

93. Which is the odd one out?

    (a) Vaccination   (b) Inoculation

    (c) Administration of medicine   (d) Digestion

94. Which is the odd one out?

    (a) Mammals   (b) Actinomycetes

    (c) Bacteria   (d) Moulds

95. Which is the odd one out?

    (a) Penicillin   (b) Health tonic

    (c) Aureomycin   (d) Chloromycetin

96. The germ theory was discovered by

    (a) Archimedes   (b) Louis Pasteur

    (c) Galileo   (d) Isaac Newton

97. Germs or bacteria can be seen

    (a) with the naked eye   (b) with a telescope

    (c) with a stethoscope   (d) with a microscope

98. The animal form of microorganisms are called

    (a) protozoa   (b) bacteria   (c) germs   (d) viruses

99. Bacteria grow and spread

    (a) by cell division

    (b) by reproduction as other animals do

    (c) by spreading like seeds as plants do

    (d) by none of these

100. The disease caused by microorganisms can be treated

    (a) by taking complete rest

(b) by antibiotics

(c) by taking a balanced diet

(d) by taking a lot of exercise in the open air.

101. Vaccination is also called

(a) germination　　　　　　　　(b) inoculation

(c) infection　　　　　　　　　(d) pasteurization

102. The Englishman who became the pioneer of vaccination was

(a) Edward Jenner　　　　　　　(b) Isaac Newton

(c) Michael Faraday　　　　　　(d) Charles Darwin

103. The man who produced vaccine against such diseases as cholera, anthrax and rabies was

(a) Marco　　　　　　　　　　(b) James Clerk Maxwell

(c) Antonie-Laurent Lavoiser　　(d) Louis Pasteur

104. What is inoculation?

105. What is pathogen?

106. What are the symptoms of typhoid?

107. What are the symptoms of leprosy?

108. What are the general symptoms of tuberculosis?

109. Who discoved the virus first of all?

110. What was the first virus to be discovered?

111. Who for the first time isolated viruses?

112. What is the substance that kills virus, called?

113. When and who discovered bacteria?

114. Who suggested the term 'bacteria' for the first time?

115. Who have been mainly instrumental in firmly establishing the germ theory of diseases?

116. How do bacteria cause diseases?

117. Which are some of the serious diseases caused by bacteria?

ALEXANDER FLEMING

118. Antibiotic medicines end in -cin. Which are some of the important antibiotic medicines?

119. Some bacteria are very dangerous and harmful while some others are very friendly and useful. How are they useful?

120. How do some bacteria help in sewage disposal?

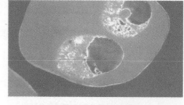

121. What are other examples to show that some bacteria are so friendly and useful?

122. What kind of infection is malaria? By which mosquito it is caused?

123. By what is malaria characterized?

124. What does malaria literally mean?

MALARIAL PARASITES IN THE RBC

125. What is the full form of TB and what bacteria cause it?

126. How are the germs of TB often introduced into our body?

127. What are the general symptoms of TB?

128. Why is TB also called consumption?

129. What is the full form of AIDS?

130. Which virus causes AIDS?

131. How is AIDS spread?

132. When was AIDS first detected?

133. What are chief symptoms of AIDS?

134. What is an anaesthetic?

135. Which are the anaesthetic gases?

136. What are the drugs used in local anaesthesia?

MORTON INHALER, A DEVICE FOR GIVING THE ANAESTHETIC

137. When was ether first used as an anaesthetic?

138. What is diagnosis?

139. What is done to detect internal disorders and diseases?

140. Why is CAT scanning becoming more popular these days?

141. What is the full form of MRI?

142. Why was primitive surgery so painful, shocking and crude?

143. When and which was the first antiseptic used by Joseph Lister?

144. When were blood types discovered?

145. Who made the first successful heart transplantation?

146. What are drugs?

147. What are the sources of drugs?

148. What is the source of antibiotic drugs?

149. What are the symptoms of cancer?

150. What is cancer?

151. How are cancer cells harmful?

1 Year   3 Years   5 Years

152. What therapies are used to treat cancer?

153. What is heart attack?

154. What is heart stroke?

155. What is the blood pressure in a normal young man?

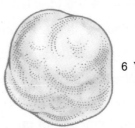

6 Years

156. What is the average life expectancy among men?

157. What is the average life expectancy among women?

GROWTH OF CANCER

158. What is the present maternal mortality rate?

159. Once a German thinker said, "The English think soap is civilizaion." How far is this remark correct?

160. Who initiated the concept of social health?

161. What have helped the modern medicine to take great strides?

162. What is molecular biology?

163. What is gene therapy?

164. What is genetic engineering?

165. What is life-parental?

166. What is autophobia?

167. What does ayurveda mean?

168. What is the basic concept of Indian medicine?

169. What is brain wash?

170. What is cardophobia?

171. What is the treatment of diseases by coloured light called?

172. Which oil obtained from a fish is very rich in vitamins A and D?

173. What is contraception?

174. What is narcotherapy?

175. What is the morbid fear and dread of one's own voice called?

176. What is polyopia?

177. What is quarantine?

178. Who first of all discovered antibiotic drug streptomycin effective against tuberculosis?

179. What are the three parts into which the small intestine is divided?

180. What is the total length of the small intestine?

181. Which of the three parts of the small intestine is the longest?

182. Why are saturated fats, if taken frequently and in large quantity, are harmful?

183. What do proteins literally mean?

184. Why roughage or fibre should be an essential part of our diet?

185. What is dermatology?

186. What is geriatics?

187. What is gynaecology?

188. What is radiotherapy?

189. Which branch of the medicine deals with the brain and nerves?

190. Which branch of medicine deals with the eyes?

191. What is anaemia?

192. What is asthama?

193. What is eczema?

194. What is bronchitis?

195. What is glaucoma?

196. What is hypothermia?

197. What is the cause of rabies?

198. Typhoid fever is a communicable disease, how is it transmitted?

199. Which type of cancer is most common among women?

200. What is acrophobia?

201. What is haptodysophoria?

202. What is entomophobia?

203. Who introduced Asprin? What are its uses?

204. Why is tetracycline taken?

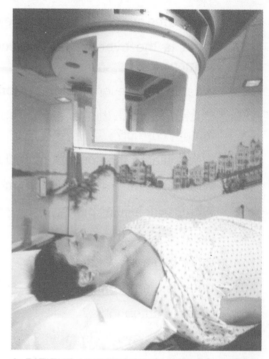

A PATIENT UNDERGOING RADIOTHERAPY

205. What is morphine?

206. What is cocaine?

207. What is the normal pulse rate of a healthy person aged 20 years at rest?

208. What is epilepsy?

209. What are sexually transmitted diseases?

210. What is psychosomatic illness?

ANSWERS

1. The practical application of anatomy helps in the diagnosis and treatment of various diseases and ailments.

2. Galen made the first detailed dissections on animals and made several discoveries about the human body.

3. Andreas Vesalius, an Italian scientist is considered the father of modern human anatomy.

4. The invention of the microscope in the 17th century revolutionised the study of human anatomy and physiology.

5. Histology is the study of human tissue etc. under a microscope.

6. Claude Bernard revealed how liver changed glycogen into glucose and regulated the sugar content of the blood. This was a significant contribution to the study of human anatomy and physiology.

7. Smallpox has now been eradicated and tuberculosis has now become curable.

8. The skeleton supports the body, anchors the muscles and protects various organs like the heart, brain, etc.

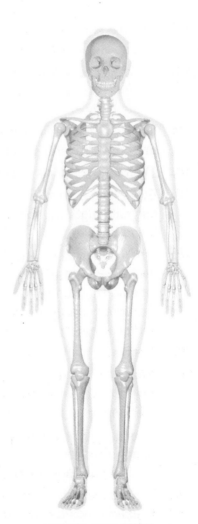

HUMAN SKELETON

9. The substance called collagen prevents bones from being brittle.

10. There is a yellow jelly-like substance in some of the bones and it is called bone-marrow where new cells are manufactured. It is an organic matter.

11. Joints are held together with ligaments which are bands of tough fibrous connective tissues.

12. The different joints found in our body are the ball and socket joints, hinge joints, angular joints, pivotal joints and gliding joints. These are all movable joints. Fibrous joints are immovable while cartilaginous joints allow only slight movement.

13. Hip and shoulder joints are good examples of ball and socket joints.

14. Muscles give a definite shape to the body and help in movement and locomotion of the various parts of the body.

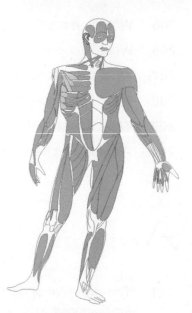

MUSCULAR SYSTEM

15. Muscle fibres are made up of thin strands made up of substances called actin and myson which lend power to muscles.

16. There are some 10 million cells in a medium-sized muscle.

17. Every time a muscle contracts to allow a movement, it must be drawn back to its original length by another contracting muscle. Which is why many muscles are found in pairs.

18. When a muscle is repeatedly contracted for long periods, its power of contraction decreases and it gets fatigued. During repeated and long periods of contraction the stored energy is used up and it does not receive as much energy as needed.

19. There are in all 639 muscles in our body.

20. Whenever there is a message from the brain a muscle may contract in less than one tenth of a second.

21. Digestion is a process by which food eaten is broken down into a form that enables our body to absorb it.

22. The organs that help in the process of digestion include the mouth, salivary glands, teeth, tongue, pharynx,

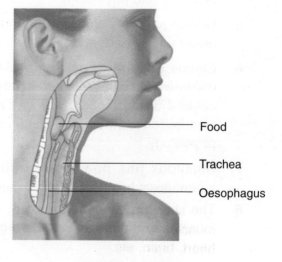

Food

Trachea

Oesophagus

HUMAN THROAT

oesophagus, liver, gall-bladder, pancreas and small and large intestines.

23. The alimentary canal joins all digestive organs together in a chain.

24. The stomach is a muscular bag which contracts and expands constantly to churn up food till it is liquid enough and easily digestible. Its function is to complete most of the process of digestion.

25. The undigested food is stored in the rectum at the lower end of the large intestine and then released as waste through the anus.

26. Human brain appears wrinkled and like a big walnut divided into two halves.

27. The cerebrum is the largest part of the human brain and is divided into two halves. The cerebrum takes about two-thirds of the brain.

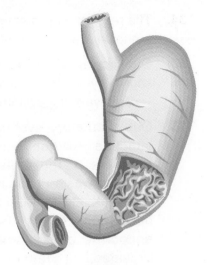

STOMACH

28. The cerebral cortex is responsible for our conscious behaviour such as perception of smell, sight, touch, hearing, ability to speak, movement of various parts of the body, thought, etc. The different parts of the cortex are responsible for different conscious activities.

29. The midbrain, pons and medulla oblongata constitute the brain stem.

30. The pons controls and regulates heart-beat, respiration, swallowing, vomiting and other vital functions.

31. Breathing is a very simple and mechanical exercise but a very vital one. While breathing we take in air into our lungs and then exhale it. When breathing in cells in our body receive oxygen. When breathing out the waste products like carbon dioxide is breathed out.

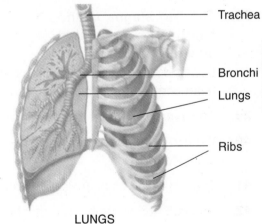

Trachea

Bronchi

Lungs

Ribs

LUNGS

32. Our lungs look like large, spongy, elastic airbags or respiratory organs that breathe in air.

33. The medulla oblongata is responsible for the control and regulation of our breathing. It accurately and exactly controls breathing according to the need of the oxygen in the body.

34. The respiratory system consists of the nose, throat (pharynx), voicebox (larynx), windpipe (trachea), the bronchi and the lungs.

35. Our circulatory system is known by another name —cardiovascular system.

36. Our circulatory system supplies oxygen and nutrients to the cells, removes waste products from the body, transports hormones from the endocrine glands and provides immune mechanism to the body. It also has clotting mechanism.

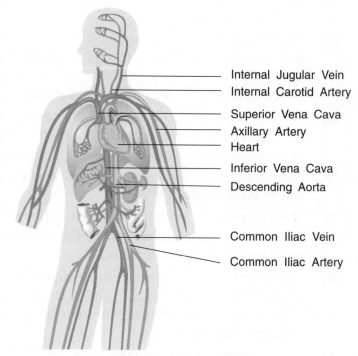

Internal Jugular Vein
Internal Carotid Artery

Superior Vena Cava
Axillary Artery
Heart

Inferior Vena Cava
Descending Aorta

Common Iliac Vein

Common Iliac Artery

THE CIRCULATORY SYSTEM

37. The two circulatory systems are the pulmonary system and the systematic system.

38. The two stages of the heart beat are called diastole and systole. During diastole the heart dilates and gets filled up with blood. During systole the heart contracts and blood is pumped out.

39. The average normal heart beat at rest is 70 to 72 beats per minute.

40. We can hear heart beat either by putting our ear against the chest or by using a stethoscope.

41. The red blood cells are of the shape of a button.

42. An adult human being carries about 6 to 6.5 litres of blood in his body.

43. Blood transports food, oxygen, hormones and antibodies to the body. It also transports waste products from the place of their origin to the place of their elimination.

44. The giant white blood cells called leucocytes, neutrophils and lymphocytes fight against diseases and provide a defence mechanism to the body.

NEUTROPHIL   LYMPHOCYTE

45. These are about 5 million red blood cells in each cubic millimetre of our blood.

46. Plasma is a clear fluid constituted mainly of water in which are dissolved proteins, antibodies, glucose, vitamins, hormones, salts, food-particles and metabolic wastes. It contains 45% red blood cells.

47. Food is a source of energy. We need energy for work, growth, repair of tissues and regulation of cellular activities and other processes. Energy is essential for the proper functioning of our body.

48. Food is burned up like a fuel in the body by combining it with oxygen. In this process food is broken down and there are a series of chemical changes. This process is called metabolism.

49. A calorie is the amount of heat required to raise the temperature of one gram of water by 1°C.

50. The calorie value of 1 gram fat is 9 calories. One gram of carbohydrate supplies 4 calories.

51. The balanced diet for an average man would contain 100 grams protein (400 calories), 100 grams fat (900 calories) and 500 gram carbohydrates (2000 calories) per day.

52. Children need more calories than aged people because they are growing and active and so can burn up the calories faster.

53. The vitamin is an organic substance found in the body in trace amounts that perform vital functions.

54. Deficiency diseases result in our body for want of vitamins.

55. Lack of vitamin B1 causes beriberi. It is found in meat, yeast, cereal, egg yolk, nuts, milk and pulses.

56. Scurvy is a deficiency disease which is caused by lack of vitamin C. It is characterized by bleeding of the tissues under the skin and from the gums.

57. Vitamin D is important for the growth and development of the bones and teeth. It is essential for children. Vitamin D is found in fish liver, butter, cheese, milk and egg. Sunlight also helps us to produce this vitamin in our body.

58. Epidermis is the outermost layer of our skin. It consists of tough and horny dead cells that protect the outer layers. It does not have any blood vessels and is waterproof.

59. The uppermost layer of our skin called the epidermis is removed at the rate at which the lower layer (basal) produces the new cells. This process goes on continuously which is why stains on our skin can be removed so easily.

60. At the bottom of the skin are chromogenes. These microorganisms produce some colours under certain conditions which give a definite colour to our skin.

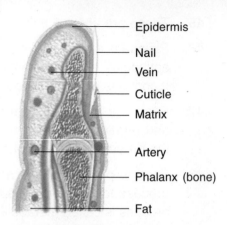

Epidermis
Nail
Vein
Cuticle
Matrix
Artery
Phalanx (bone)
Fat

NAIL STRUCTURE

61. Our nails are lifeless and epidermal derivatives. They have keratin to make them more hard and horny. They are not connected with nerves, nor do they have blood cells. Therefore, we do not feel pain when we cut our nails.

62. Sunlight can produce the black pigment called melanin in our skin.

63. Our eye is like a video camera which has an adjustable window called pupil to let in light. It has a lens in the form of the dark spot in front of the eye. It has the retina which works like a sensitive film on which images are formed. The cornea protects the eye while the iris regulates the size of the pupil.

64. When light enters the eye, an upside down image is formed on the sensitive retina. The sensors of the retina send nerve impulses to the brain through the optic nerve. Then the brain interprets the message and the object is seen as an image.

65. The light sensitive retina is made up of some 130 million cells. These are called rods and cones. They send messages to the brain through the optic nerve. Rod-cells are sensitive to very dim-light but cannot distinguish colours. Cones can distinguish between colours but are not sensitive to light as rods are.

66. The three kinds of cone cells distinguish between colours. One is sensitive to red light, another to blue and the third to green. They are photosensitive and work only in good light.

69. The nose is an organ at the front of our face. It is used for breathing, smelling and to some extent for producing nasal sounds.

70. The smell receptors are located behind the olfactory bulb in the epithelium and line the upper nasal cavity. These very sensitive tiny tissues or cells number about 5 million.

71. The tiny group of olfactory receptors are responsible for our sense of smell. They pick up some of the molecules in the air passing over them and react against them.

67. Some animals like the elephant, deer, hare, etc. have big outer ears, which they can easily move. These big outer ears help them to catch even the slightest sound.

68. When the sound wave enters the ear and strikes the ear drum, the ear drums begin to vibrate rapidly. It makes the three little bones rattle. These bones touch

Chapter 7

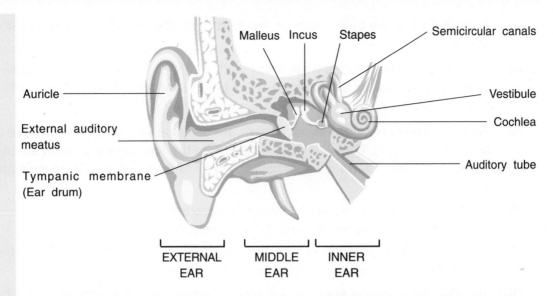

both the ear drum and the inner ear and are called oscilles. Oscilles create vibrations in the tube of the inner ear which is filled with a fluid called cochlea. Cochlea converts these vibrations into nerve impulses which are carried to the brain. The brain recognises and interprets these waves into sound.

72. Teeth are used for biting, cutting, chiselling, mastication and chewing of food. These are also used for gnawing, digging and fighting.

Chapter 7

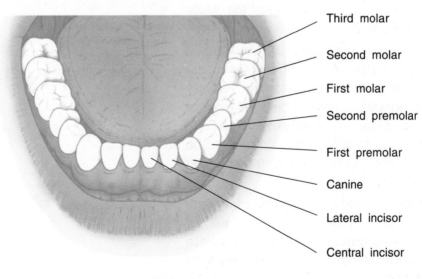

HUMAN DENTURE

73. The tooth gets its nourishment through the root-canal which is at the base of the root. Through this canal pass the nerves and blood-vessels. These carry the

nourishment to the pulp cavity of the tooth and also waste products out of the structure.

74. Collective dentition means a full set of teeth with four different kinds of teeth—the incisors, the cuspids, the molar and the pre-molar-teeth. They perform different types of functions.

75. We should be very careful in our dental care because we human beings have only two-series of teeth. One is milk teeth and then the final series of teeth about the age of 12. But the lower animals have a series of succession of teeth throughout their life.

76. DNA or deoxyribonucleic acid contains genetic information in most living beings. Every human cell has nearly 2 mt. DNA supercoiled on itself.

77. The basis of classification of human blood are the proteins found in red blood corpuscles and specific antibodies formed in serum.

78. The four blood groups are A, B, AB and O. Persons with A group blood can have blood from A and O groups, and those with B can have from B and O groups. The people with AB blood group can have blood from another group. Those with O group can have blood only from O group.

79. An American pathologist and Nobal laureate Karl Landsteiner suggested these four blood groups for the first time in 1900. Blood tranfusion is a process by which lost or destroyed blood is replaced intravenously with compatible citrated human blood. Before blood transfusion, blood groups are determined. The recipient and the donor should belong to the same blood group.

80. Dialysis is a technique by which blood is filtered through membrane to remove waste products. It is performed naturally by kidneys. In case of damged kidneys it is done artificially by a special machine. Now damaged kidneys can be removed and healthy one transplanted instead.

81. A sweat gland is a coiled, tubular gland embeded in dermis. The function of sweat glands is to excrete waste material and excess of water in the form of sweat.

82. A finger is one of the five digits of the hand. Every finger and thumb has a series of groves and ridges. This pattern

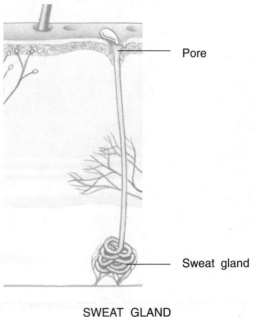

Pore

Sweat gland

SWEAT GLAND

of grooves and ridges is so unique that no two individuals can have the identical finger-patterns or prints. These remain the same from birth till death. When fingers come into contact with some suitable surface, they leave their impressions and imprints.

83. A twin is one of the two born at birth. The twins are very much alike to each other. Identical twins are born when a single fertilized egg produces two embroys which develop into two babies.

84. Good health depends on both chance and choice. What we inherit is a matter of chance. But there are many choices which determine how healthy we are.

85. Puberty is the age when reproductive organs become functionally active. In girls it is earlier than in the boys.

86. Adolescence is the pre-adult period of life of a man or woman. It is the period between 12-13 to 18-19 years of age. Rapid changes take place during this period which include both physical and psychological.

87. Menopause in women occur when there is cessation of menstrual periods. It is a stage when the ovaries get exhausted and start shrinking.

88. Asexual reproduction is more common in plants and vegetation than in animal life. However, some of the lower animals reproduce by simple division. In plants new plants are produced from various parts of old plants.

89. (d)	**90.** (b)	**91.** (d)	**92.** (c)	**93.** (d)	**94.** (a)
95. (b)	**96.** (b)	**97.** (d)	**98.** (a)	**99.** (a)	**100.** (b)
101. (b)	**102.** (a)	**103.** (d)			

104. Inoculation involves introduction of virus or other organism of a disease into blood for curative or experimental purpose.

105. Pathogen is a virus, micro-organism, other living or non-living agent that can cause disease in a body.

106. Typhoid spreads by contaminated food, faeces and carriers. The symptoms of typhoid are fever, nausea, vomiting, severe abdominal pain, chills and diarrhoea.

107. Leprosy affects the patient's skin and causes ulcers, deformities of fingers and toes. The affected areas become senseless and eyebrows begin falling off.

108. The general symptoms of tuberculosis are hectic fever, sweating and emaciation.

109. D. Iwanoswki discovered the virus first of all.

110. The first virus to be discovered was higher plant virus.

111. W.M. Stanley isolated the viruses for the first time.

112. The substance that kills virus is called viricide.

113. Anton Van Leeuwenhock discovered bacteria in 1676.

114. Ehrenberg was the first to suggest the term 'bacteria.

115. French chemist Louis Pasteuer (1822-1895) and German doctor Robert Koch (1843-1910) have been mainly responsible for firmly establishing the germ theory of diseases.

LOUIS PASTEUER

116. Bacteria cause many diseases which are very serious by producing toxins due to the decomposition of living protoplasm.

117. Some serious diseases caused by bacteria include pneumonia, tuberculosis, leprosy, cholera, jaundice. etc.

118. Some important antibiotic medicines are ;

Chloromycetin, Aureomycin, Streptomycin, Terramycin, Bracitracin, Neomycin.

119. Some bacteria are really very useful. For example, many of the bacteria make soil fertile by converting ammonium compounds into nitrites and nitrites into nitrates.

120. Many bacteria are very helpful in the final disposal of sewage. The sewage contain solid and semi-solid waste. Bacteria break down the solid matter and decompose the organic matter into very simple compounds. The sludge thus produced is used as manure.

121. The other examples of bacteria's usefulness and friendliness are curd and vinegar. Curd is a very useful product of bacteria, similarly some bacteria help in converting alcohol into vinegar.

122. Malaria is a protozoan infection. It is caused by the female anopheles mosquito.

123. Malaria is characterized by recurring chills, high fever, shivering and anaemia.

124. The word "malaria" is Italian and means "bad/poisonous air" because it was believed that it was caused by poisonous air of the swamps. And swamps are the home and breeding ground of the anopheles mosquito.

125. The full form of TB is tuberculosis and it is caused by the tubercle bacillus.

126. TB germs are often introduced into our lungs through breathing. In the initial stage it is called primary lesion.

127. The general symptoms of TB are hectic fever, sweating, cough and emaciation.

128. TB is also called consumption because it slowly and steadily wastes away the whole body; the patient becomes lean, thin and weak and ultimately dies if proper and timely treatment is not given.

129. The full form of AIDS is Acquired Immune Deficiency Syndrome.

130. AIDS is caused by Human Immuno-deficiency Virus a retrovirus that directly attacks and destroys the body's natural defence mechanism.

131. AIDS is often spread by casual sex with strangers, anal sex and blood transfusion. Sharing injection with drug-addicts or using unsterilised needle for vaccination are other causes of spread of AIDS.

132. First case of AIDS was detected in New York in 1981.

133. The chief symptoms of AIDS are enlargement of lymph nodes, slight fever, chronic diarrhoea, significant weight loss, etc.

134. An anaesthetic is a substance used in medicine to create insensibility or loss of feeling. It is used to control pain.

135. The anaesthetic gases are nitrous oxide, chloroform, ether and ethylene.

136. Local anaesthetics include eucaine, cocaine, novacaine, etc.

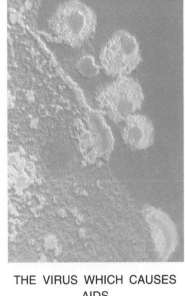

THE VIRUS WHICH CAUSES AIDS

137. Ether was first used as an anaesthetic in 1846.

138. Diagnosis is the identification and detection of a disease by means of its symptoms. It is necessary for proper treatment and health care.

139. Scanning and medical imaging are undertaken to detect internal disorders and diseases. For this purpose ultrasound, computerized axial tomography (CAT) scanning and ecocardiography are used.

140. CAT scanning is becoming more popular these days because it provides detailed cross-sectional and three-dimensional images of the internal organs.

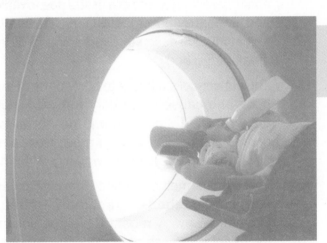

CAT SCAN MACHINES ALLOW THE DOCTORS TO SEE INSIDE THE BODY WITHOUT CUTTING IT OPEN.

141. The full form of MRI is magnetic resonance imaging.

142. Primitive surgery was very painful, crude and shocking because of the lack of antiseptics, anaesthetics and inadequate knowledge about the human anatomy. It killed more people than it saved. The shock of the operation often killed the patient.

143. Joseph Lister used carbolic acid for the first time as an antiseptic in 1867.

144. The blood types were discovered in 1900. Surgical operations further improved with it because it made blood transfusion possible.

145. The first successful heart transplantation was done by the South African physician Christian Bernard in 1967.

146. A drug is a substance that affects functioning of a living organism. It is used for the prevention, diagnosis and treatment of diseases.

147. Drugs are obtained from animals, plants and minerals. They can also be produced synthetically.

148. Antibiotic drugs are obtained from moulds. Penicillin and streptomycin are examples of such type of drugs.

149. The symptoms of cancer include some unusual lump in the body, specially in the chest, a sore near the mouth, repeated bouts of indigestion, change in size and colour of moles or worts, hoarseness of voice and unusual discharge or bleeding from any body opening.

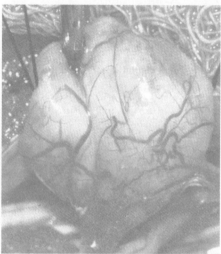

150. Cancer is a malignant continuous growth and abnormal enlargement of a tissue due to rapid and uncontrolled cell division. The cells forming the disease start spreading to other areas of the body.

TUMOR OF THE SPINAL CORD

151. The cancer cells migrate to other parts of the body and cause secondary tumors. They grow rapidly by division and do not allow normal and healthy cells to grow, work and remain alive. They interfere in the working of normal cells.

152. The various methods used to treat cancer include surgical methods, radiation therapy and chemotherapy. A recent development in cancer treatment is the use of monoclonal antibodies

153. The malfunctioning of the heart because of the arteries becoming narrow, blood-clotted, blocked or hemorrhaged is called heart attack.

154. When the supply of blood is cut off to any part of the brain for whatever reason, there is a heart stroke. It

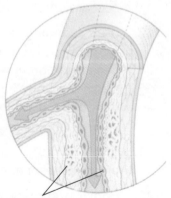

Fatty-plaque

CORONARY ARTERY

affects the other parts of the brain as well and the result is death in most of the cases.

155. The blood pressure in a normal young man is 120/80. With age the blood pressure gradually climbs up and is 140/87 by the age of 60.

156. The average life expectancy among men is 65 years.

157. The average life expectancy among women is 67 years.

158. The present maternal mortality rate is 307 children after every 1000 maternity cases.

159. The German thinker was right when he said soap is civilization. Social and personal health is a matter of good sanitation to a large extent and soap has helped us a lot in creating hygienic and healthful conditions.

160. Edwin Chadwick initiated the concept of social health by emphasizing the need and importance of control and eradication of the causes of disease.

EDWIN CHADWICK

161. Modern medicine has taken great strides because of discovery of germs by Louis Pasteuer, of antiseptics by Joseph Lister, of vaccination by Edward Jenner, of anesthetics by Charles Jackson, of blood groups and antibiotic drugs by Alexander Flemming.

162. Molecular biology is a branch of science which investigates biological processes at the molecular level.

163. Gene therapy is the treatment of diseases caused by defective genes. A gene is a hereditary factor carried on chromosomes in cell nuclie passed from generation to generation.

164. Genetic engineering is a very comprehensive term. It includes all investigations and efforts made in changing the genetic code for ever by manipulating the genes.

165. Life-parental is an average period of 40-41 weeks between conception and birth.

166. Autophobia is pathological self hatred. It also means extreme dread of solitude.

167. Ayurveda means the Science of Life. It is Indian system of medicine. It implies both the science of living and art of living.

168. The basic concept of Indian medicine is the doctrine of humours (dosha). It believed that the health can be maintained through the even balance of the three vital fluids— wind gall, mucus and blood.

169. Brain-wash means keeping a person under long systematic pressure by various means with a view to get his mind, ideas, concepts etc. changed.

170. Cardophobia is a morbid fear of heart disease and disorders.

171. The treatment of diseases by coloured light is called chromotherapy.

172. Codliver oil is very rich in vitamins A and D which ensure good health of skin and bones. It is obtaind from the fresh liver of codfish.

173. Contraception is a method of birth-control. It undertakes prevention of conception or pregnancy usually by artificial means.

174. Narcotherapy is a treatment of disturbed mental state by means of prolonged drug induced sleep.

175. The morbid fear and dread of one's own voice is called Phonophobia.

176. Polyopia is perception of several images of the same object.

177. Quarantine is isolation of infected or suspected person in order to prevent the spread of that disease.

178. It was Selman A. Waksman of the US who discovered streptomycin, the first antibiotic medicine against tuberculosis.

179. The small intestine is divided into duodenum, jefunam and ilium.

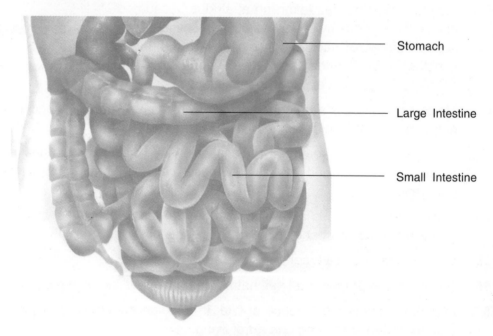

Stomach

Large Intestine

Small Intestine

THE INTESTINES

180. The total length of small intestine is 8.62 metres.

181. The third part called ilium is the longest and measures 3.65 mt.

182. Saturated fats, if taken frequently and in large quantity, are harmful because they increase the level of serum cholesterol.

183. Protein literally means "first in importance". It is derived from the Greek word 'protelos' which means first or prime. Proteins are composed of essential amino acids.

184. Roughage or fibre should form an essential part of our diet because it helps in removal of constipation. It also helps in the easy movement of the intestines. Fibre-diet also reduces the intake of food and thereby result in quick and proper digestion. Fibre-rich diet tends to lower the blood-pressure and blood cholesterol.

185. Dermatology is the branch of medicine which deals with skin.

186. Geriatics is the branch of medicine which deals with old people.

187. Gynaecology is the branch of medicine which deals with the female reproductive organs.

188. Radiotherapy is the branch of medicine which deals with x-rays.

189. Neurology is the branch of medicine that deals with brain and nerves.

190. Opthalmology is the branch of medicine which deals with eyes.

191. Anaemia is deficiency of haemoglobin in red blood-cells.

192. Asthama is a disease of the respiratory system that causes difficulty in breathing.

193. Eczema is infection of the skin which causes blisters and scaling.

194. Bronchitis is inflammation of bronchi.

195. Glaucoma is the disease of the eye which causes high blood pressure in the eye's fluid, pain and partial or total loss of vision.

196. Hypothermia involves serious loss of body heat. The symptoms of hypothermia are drowsiness, confusion, pallor etc. If not cured in the time it may lead to unconsciousness and even death.

197. A virus causes rabies which may be transmitted by a bite of rabid animal.

198. Typhoid fever is transmitted through contaminated food and water.

199. Breast cancer is very common among women.

200. Acrophobia is morbid fear of height and high places.

201. Haptodysophoria is an unpleasant sensation derived from touching certain objects.

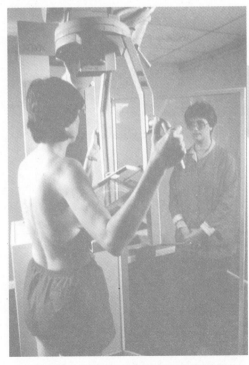

A WOMAN HAVING A MAMMOGRAPHY, AN X-RAY THAT CHECKS FOR BREAST CANCER

202. Entomophobia is aversion to or extreme and morbid fear of insects.

203. Asprin was introduced in 1893 by Hermann Dresser. It relieves pain, reduces fever and prevents blood-clotting.

204. Tetracycline is taken to treat pneumonia, bronchitis and chest infections.

205. Morphine relieves severe pain. It is derived from opium and causes addiction if taken regularly.

206. Cocaine is much abused drug. Its addiction causes increased heart-beat and blood-pressure, anxiety, insommia, weightloss and prschosis.

207. The normal pulse rate of a healthy person aged 20, at rest is 71 beats per minute.

208. Epilepsy is a chronic functional disease of nervous system. It causes recurring attacks of sudden and violent unconsiousness.

209. AIDS, gonorrhoea etc. are sexually transmitted diseases.

210. Psychosomatic illness is a condition caused or worsened by psychological factors.

Chapter 8

DISCOVERIES & INVENTIONS

$\mathcal{Q}$UESTIONS

Read the following statements quickly and say if each of these is True or False. Answers follow.

1. Glass is one of the most useful man-made materials. True/False.

2. To manufacture glass, sand, soda ash or potash and lime are needed. True/False.

3. Glass-making could have been discovered in one country only. True/False

4. The ancient Egyptians, Mesopotamians and Phoenicians did not know how to make glass 5,000 years ago before the Christian Era. True/False.

5. By 300 B.C. Alexandrians achieved the skills in moulding glass into a number of shapes. True/False.

6. The skill of shaping molten glass by blowing through a pipe was developed in China. True/False.

7. By the early 18th century the use of glass-sheets for windows by the common people became a usual thing in many countries including England. True/False.

8. There are only a few kinds of plastics. True/False.

9. Plastics are polymers made up of lots of monomers. True/False.

10. Cellulose could not be moulded and bent. True/False.

11. Celluloid was produced by John Hyatt which could be used in place of ivory. True/False

12. Phenolic plastics was discovered by Leo Backeland in 1970. True/False

13. Plastics are not pollutants. True/False

14. Plastics cause serious environmental damage by accumulating in the environment. True/False

15. Plastic is a substance that cannot be easily shaped and formed into many different shapes. True/False

16. Vaccination was discovered by an English physician called Edward Jenner. False/True

17. Jenner took some fluid from a blister of his body and introduced it into the skin of a boy. False/True

18. In vaccination a dose is administered of a disease too small to do any harm but sufficient to activate the body in producing antibodies for that particular disease. The antibodies invade and eliminate the germs. False/True

EDWARD JENNER

19. Vaccination is called passive immunisation. False/True

20. By the use of vaccination smallpox has been totally eradicated and many infectious diseases like whooping cough, tetanus, polio etc. have been effectively controlled to a great extent. False/True

21. Bakelite, a synthetic resin, has been named after its inventor Leo Hendrick Baekeland. False/True

22. Bakelite is used to produce synthetic drugs and colours. False/True

23. Roger Bacon was the first person to suggest of a man flying sitting amidst a flying machine. False/True

24. Man first experienced flying in the air by means of balloons filled with gas or hot air. False/True

25. American Wright Brothers were the first to take to air on 17th December, 1903 in their home-made winged aircraft. False/True

GEORGE CAYLEY

26. A flight across the English Channel took place for the first time in 1909 by Louis Bleriot. False/True

27. George Cayley of France is believed to have made a steam helicopter in 1796. False/True

28. In 1909 Igor Sikorsky made a helicopter which could lift itself successfully in space. False/True

29. The helicopter made by the German company Focke Wulf could fly at the speed of 200 miles per hour. False/True

30. The steampowered engine made by Nicolas Cugnot in 1769 was quite successful. True/False.

31. Etinne Lenoir made an engine which was a practical one like found in modern cars. True/False

32. The first motor car engines were mounted on horse-carts. True/False

33. By 1908 production of cars on mass scale began when Model T Ford started to be manufactured in America. True/False

34. The first steam engine was used to draw water from the wells for irrigation. True/False

35. In 1825 George Stephenson started the first passenger railway in England run by a steam engine. True/False

FORD-T

STEAM ENGINE BUILT BY GEORGE STEPHENSON

36. Richard Trevithick who was the first to create a steam engine was a German. True/False

37. A live electric rail running parallel to the railway track is called the third track. True/False

38. The first high speed train was made in France. True/False

39. Dynamite was invented by a Swedish chemist Alfred Nobel. True/False.

40. Is microscope a wonderful instrument? Yes/No

41. Has the use of ordinary magnifying glass started recently? Yes/No

42. When we talk of the invention of the microscope do we mean the compound microscope? Yes/No

43. Was miscroscope invented in 300 B.C.? Yes/No

44. The study of anatomy on the microscopic scale is called histology? Yes/No

45. Leeuwenhoek was the first person to observe the unicellular organisms through a microscope in the 1670s. Yes/No

46. Did Robert Hook saw tiny spaces throughout a sample of cork and called them cells? Yes/No

EARLY MICROSCOPE

47. Are atoms stationary? Yes/No

48. Does physics deal with disease and their treatment? Yes/No

49. Does the term "atom" mean "undivisible" in Greek? Yes/No

50. Was it an English scientist who first proposed the atomic theory of matter in 1803? Yes/No

51. Can nitrogen nuclei be converted into oxygen nuclei? Yes/No

52. Is the mass of an electron less than that of an atom? Yes/No

53. Can some 60,000 stars be seen by the naked eye? Yes/No

54. Is an optical telescope used for viewing microorganisms? Yes/No

55. Are only two lenses used in a refracting telescope? Yes/No

56. Do the stars look twinkling because of the atmospheric disturbance of the earth? Yes/No

57. Was Galileo the first scientist to make use of a telescope? Yes/No

58. Does the planet Saturn have rings? Yes/No

59. Was it Edwin Hubble who said that the universe was larger than had been imagined? Yes/No

60. Which is the odd one out?

(a) Microscope   (b) Telescope

(c) Camera   (d) Stethoscope

61. Which is the odd one out?

(a) Film   (b) Cellulose   (c) Plastic   (d) Cement

62. Which is the odd one out?

(a) Book   (b) Video camera   (c) Lens   (d) Exposure

63. Which is the odd one out?

(a) Copies   (b) Kodak

(c) Steel company   (d) Film Company

64. Which is the odd one out?

(a) TV set   (b) Einstein   (c) John Baird   (d) Vladimir

65. Which is the odd one out?

(a) Broadcast   (b) Ocean

(c) Electrical Impulses   (d) Screen

66. Which is the odd one out?

(a) Zero   (b) Calculation   (c) Numbers   (d) Rain forest

67. Which is the odd one out?

(a) Subtraction   (b) Division   (c) Examination   (d) Multiplication

68. Which is the odd one out?

(a) Mathematician   (b) Calculator

(c) Zero   (d) Horse-riding

69. Which is the odd one out?

(a) Digits   (b) Anatomy   (c) Bhaskara   (d) Place value

70. Which is the odd one out?

(a) Numerology   (b) Symbols   (c) Algebra   (d) Civics

71. Who invented the metric system of weights and measures?

(a) Aristotle   (b) French Academy

(c) UNO   (d) Charles Darwin

72. What does "metre" in Latin mean?

(a) Book   (b) Measure

(c) Depth   (d) Flight of a bird

73. When was an international conference held in Washington, USA to evolve a uniform time zone?

(a) 1990   (b) 1970   (c) 1750   (d) 1884

74. In how many time zones has the world been divided?

(a) 12   (b) 24   (c) 36   (d) 9

75. What is the time difference between one zone and the next?

(a) 1 hour   (b) 30 minutes   (c) 24 hours   (d) 2 hours

76. How much advance is Indian standard time (IST) of Greenwich Mean Time (GMT)?

(a) 5 hours   (b) 5 hours and 30 minutes

(c) 4 hours   (d) 6 hours

77. Through which place does the prime meridian (0° longitude) pass?

(a) London   (b) New York   (c) Delhi   (d) Tokyo

78. What function did diodes perform as valves?

(a) Magnified the sound

(b) Permitted current to pass only one way

(c) Changed light into electric impulses

(d) Made devices long lasting

79. In which year was the transistor invented?

(a) 1870   (b) 1900

(c) 1947   (d) 1857

TYPES OF TRANSISTORS

80. What made the electronic devices so small, compact and more cheap?

(a) Diodes   (b) Triodes

(c) Transistors   (d) None of these

81. Where is the hormone insulin produced is the human body?

(a) Pancreas

(b) Liver

(c) Stomach

(d) Kidney

82. When was the term "hormone" first coined?

(a) 1920   (b) 1905

(c) 1925   (d) 1926

INSULIN SECRETARY GLAND

83. Who identified and isolated insulin for the first time ?
    (a) Richard Owen
    (b) Leibniz
    (c) Francis Baily
    (d) Fredrick Grant Banting

84. For which disease is insulin used?
    (a) Tuberculosis
    (b) Diabetes
    (c) Paralysis
    (d) Common cold

85. What does insulin do when administered in the body of a diabetic patient?
    (a) Relives blood pressure
    (b) Relieves pain
    (c) Reduces blood sugar
    (d) Removes weakness

86. Who invented the calendar?
    (a) The Indians
    (b) The Egyptians
    (c) The Phoenicians
    (d) The Chinese

87. What did the wise men of Egypt observe each year before the flooding of the river Nile?
    (a) A certain star rose before the sun set
    (b) The Sun looked blue at rising
    (c) The crocodiles appeared in the River Nile
    (d) The day and night were of equal length

88. How much time does the Earth take to make a complete round of the Sun?
    (a) 365.256 days
    (b) 360 days
    (c) 366 days
    (d) 365 days

89. What is the speed of the Earth?
    (a) 5,000 km/h
    (b) 2,000 km/h
    (c) 1,600 km/h
    (d) 2,500 km/h

90. How many days were dropped from the year 1582 by Pope Gregory XIII?
    (a) 9 days
    (b) 10 days
    (c) 7 days
    (d) 15 days

91. What are the two halves in which Hindu month is divided?
    (a) First half and second half
    (b) The bright half and the dark half
    (c) The good half and the bad half
    (d) The Man's half and the Gods' half

92. Which famous lady is said to have invented the war-like game of chess?

    (a) Kunti, the mother of the Pandava princes.

    (b) Mandodari, the wife of Ravana

    (c) Savitri, the wife of Satyavan

    (d) Parvati, the consort of Shiva

93. What does the term "Chaturanga" in Sanskrit mean?

    (a) The four directions: East, West, North and South

    (b) The four wheels of a chariot

    (c) The four limbs of the ancient Indian army

    (d) The four pillars of a structure

94. Who is said to have taught chess to the Pandava and Kaurava princess?

    (a) Dronacharya

    (b) Bhishma Pitamaha

    (c) Maharishi Vyasa

    (d) Shakuni

CHESS BOARD

95. In which country was chess invented?

    (a) India   (b) Arabia   (c) Persia   (d) Russia

96. In which year did a Scottish blacksmith named Kirkpatric Macmillan make a bicycle?

    (a) 1850   (b) 1839   (c) 1900   (d) 1890

97. Who developed the modern safety bicycle and when?

    (a) James Starley in 1870s   (b) Wright Brothers in 1990s

    (c) J.L. Baird in 1890s   (d) Charles Goodyear in 1840s

98. Who invented the telephone and when ?

99. What does a telephone instrument consist of?

100. How does the telephone work?

101. What is a refrigerator?

102. Who discovered for the first time how to change ammonia vapour to a liquid by compressing it?

103. Who syntherized the first wholly artificial gene?

104. Who discovered the planet uranus?

105. Who coined the term 'ecology?'

106. Why was Alberst Einstein given the Nobel Prize in 1921?

107. Why is John Dalton known?

108. Who devised a temperature scale based on the freezing and boiling points of water?

109. Why is Marie Curie famous?

110. Who discovered Ohm's law?

111. Who discovered the method of making a magnet?

112. Who for the first time used the term "hormone".

113. Who coined the term "chemotherapy?"

114. For what is the Greek thinker Euclid best known?

115. Who discovered nuclear fission?

116. What is the full name of the astronomer after whom Halley's comet has been named?

117. What is "Hippocratic Oath?"

118. Who was the famous Indian surgeon in 2nd century BC?

119. Who devised the Richter Scale?

120. Who gave us the theory of continental drift?

121. Who were the husband and wife to prove that humans evolved in Africa and quite earlier than was supposed?

122. Who invented the elevator?

123. Who was the first to reach the North Pole?

124. Who discovered the mighty Victoria Falls (Zimbabwe)?

125. Who made the first printing press?

126. Who discovered Alaska?

127. Who started the Red Cross?

NUCLEAR FISSION

128. Who discovered Greenland?

129. Who invented the atom bomb and when?

130. Who invented bakelite?

131. Who invented stainless steel?

132. By whom were germs of malaria discovered?

133. Who used psychoanalysis for the first time?

134. Who invented electro-cardiography?

135. Who discovered DDT?

136. Who discovered insulin?

137. Who discovered CAT scanner?

138. Who produced first Test Tube Baby?

139. Who invented the sewing machine?

140. Who discovered vulcanised rubber?

141. By whom was safety razor invented?

142. Who invented neon lamp?

143. Who invented gramophone?

144. Fountain pen was discovered by Lewis E. Waterman. To which country did he belong?

145. Who invented cinema?

146. Who invented barometer?

147. Who invented the ballistic missile?

148. Who discovered celluloid?

149. By whom was digital computer invented?

150. Who invented electric welding?

GRAMOPHONE

$\mathcal{A}$NSWERS

1. True	**2.** True.	**3.** False	**4.** False	**5.** True	**6.** False
7. True	**8.** False	**9.** True	**10.** False	**11.** True	**12.** True
13. False	**14.** True	**15.** False	**16.** True	**17.** False	**18.** True

19. False	**20.** True	**21.** True	**22.** False	**23.** True	**24.** True
25. True	**26.** True	**27.** True	**28.** True	**29.** False	**30.** False
31. True	**32.** True	**33.** True	**34.** False	**35.** True	**36.** False
37. True	**38.** False	**39.** True	**40.** Yes	**41.** No	**42.** Yes
43. No	**44.** Yes	**45.** Yes	**46.** Yes	**47.** No	**48.** No
49. Yes	**50.** Yes	**51.** Yes	**52.** Yes	**53.** No	**54.** No
55. Yes	**56.** Yes	**57.** Yes	**58.** Yes	**59.** Yes	**60.** (d)
61. (d)	**62.** (a)	**63.** (c)	**64.** (b)	**65.** (b)	**66.** (d)
67. (c)	**68.** (d)	**69.** (b)	**70.** (d)	**71.** (b)	**72.** (b)
73. (d)	**74.** (b)	**75.** (a)	**76.** (b)	**77.** (a)	**78.** (b)
79. (c)	**80.** (c)	**81.** (a)	**82.** (b)	**83.** (d)	**84.** (b)
85. (c)	**86.** (b)	**87.** (a)	**88.** (a)	**89.** (c)	**90.** (b)
91. (b)	**92.** (b)	**93.** (c)	**94.** (c)	**95.** (a)	**96.** (b)
97. (a)					

98. Alexander Graham Bell invented the telephone in 1876 in Boston, America.

99. A telephone instrument consists of a transmitter (mouthpiece), a receiver (ear piece) and a dial mechanism or push-button facility.

A MODERN TELEPHONE INSTRUMENT

100. When we speak in the mouthpiece, the sound waves strike an aluminium disk or diaphragm which converts them into electric waves and at the other end of the receiver the aluminium disk starts vibrating exactly as does the disk in the transmitter. And the electric waves are converted into sound waves and we hear the voice of the speaker.

Mouth-piece

Receiver

Dial

DIAL TYPE TELEPHONE INSTRUMENT

101. A refrigerator is a device used for keeping food and other things cool and fresh.

102. It was Michael Faraday who discovered how to change ammonia vapour to a liquid by compressing it and then removing heat from it. When the pressure is removed and the liquid is allowed to evaporate again, it removes heat and produces cold.

103. Indian-born US citizen and Nobel Laureate synthesized the first wholly artificial gene.

104. Willion Herschell, a German astronomer discovered the planet Uranus.

105. Sihidy Hacckal (184-1819), a German biologist coined the term 'ecology'. He coined this term after long and wide ranging experiments and researches in botany and zoology.

106. Albert Einstein (1879-1955) was a German-born US citizen and famous scientist. He was given Nobel Prize for his theory of relativity.

107. John Dalton (1766-1844) was a British Scientist who put forward the modern atomic theory. He is well known for his discovery of the law of partial pressure now known as Dalton's Law.

JOHN DALTON

108. A Swedish astronomer Anders Celsius devised the temperature scale on which water freezes at zero degree and boils at hundred degrees. It was once called centigrade scale but was later renamed as Celsius Scale in 1948.

109. Marie Curie (1867-1934) was a famous French chemist and physicist who discovered radio-active element radium. She was given Noble Prize twice, one in 1903 and then again in 1911.

110. Georg Simon Ohm (1789-1845) was a German physicist. He discovered Ohm's Law which shows the relationship between potential difference and current.

111. William Gilbert (1544-1603) an English physicist discovered the method of making a magnet by stroking an iron bar with a permanent magnet.

112. Hormones are natural organic substances which regulate, growth metabolism and other functions of an organism. William Maddock Bayliss (1860-1934) was an English physiologist to use the term "hormone" for the first time.

113. A German biologist Paul Ehrlich, who made significant contribution to the study of blood and imune system, coined the term "chemo-therapy".

114. Euclid was a great Greek thinker and mathematician and is best known for his fundamental work on geometry.

115. Otto Han the German physicist with Fritz Strassmann discovered nuclear fission in which an atomic nucleus splits

OTTO HAN

into nearly two equal fragments with the release of large amount of energy.

EDMUND HALLEY

116. Edmund Halley first calculated the Comet's orbit round the sun after whom Halley's Comet has been named. It takes about 76 years to orbit around the sun and was last seen in 1986. He calculated and discovered that some comets return on a regular basis.

117. The doctors take an oath after the completion of their studies that binds them to a certain code of conduct. This oath is known "Hippocratic Oath." It has been named so in the memory of an ancient Greek physician Hippocrates.

118. Shushruta was a famous Indian surgeon and physician of 2nd century BC. He studied extensively all sides of medicine and surgery of that time.

119. Richter Scale measures the energy released by an earthquake. Earth scientists use it to detect and compare the magnitude and potential destructive power of earthquakes. This scale was devised by an American seismologist named Charles Francis Richter (1900-1985) along with Beno Gutenberg.

120. The theory of continental drift says that the present location of continental masses is the result of fragmentation of one or more pre-existing land-masses. A German scientist Alfred Wegner (1890-1930) originated this theory.

121. The English couple (husband and wife) Louis Leakey and Mary Leakey proved by their archaeological researches that human beings evolved in Africa quite earlier than was supposed.

122. The elevator was invented by Elisha Otis. But the modern electric elevator was later developed by the German engineer Werner von Siemens.

123. Admiral Robert E Peary of the US was the first man to reach the North Pole on April 16, 1909.

124. David Livingstone, an English missionary and scholar, discovered the mighty Victoria Falls.

125. Johann Gutenberg of Germany was the first person to make use of the printing press. He printed the first book, the famous Gutenbergs Bible.

126. In 1741 Alaska was discovered by two men, one Dane and another Russian. They landed on the mainland of Alaska in separate ships in an expedition to that land. The Dane was Bering and the Russian Alexeichirkov.

Chapter 8

126. In 1741 Alaska was discovered by two men, one Dane and another Russian. They landed on the mainland of Alaska in separate ships in an expedition to that land. The Dane was Bering and the Russian Alexeichirkov.

127. The Red Cross was started in 1864 by the great humanitarian efforts of a Swiss gentleman called Henri Dunant.

128. Greenland was discovered by an Icelander called Eric the Red in 982.

129. Atom bomb was discovered in 1945 by J.R. Oppenhaimer in the USA.

130. Bakelite was invented by Leo Bakeland in 1907 in Belgium.

J.R. OPPENHAIMER

131. Stainless steel was invented by Harry Brearley in 1913.

132. Malaria germs were discovered by Laveran in France in 1880.

133. Signmund Freud of Austria used psychoanalysis in 1895 for the first time.

134. Electro-cardiograph was invented by Willem Einthoven of Netherland.

135. DDT (Dichloro-Diphenyl-Trichloroethane) was invented by Edward Calvin-Kendall of the US in 1936.

136. Banting and Best of Canada discovered insulin in 1921.

137. CAT scanner was invented by Godfrey Hounsfield of Britain in 1968.

138. First Test Tube Baby was produced in 1978 by Steptoe and Edwards in Britain.

139. Sewing machine was invented in 1829 by Barthelemy Thimmonnier of France.

140. Vulcanised rubber was discovered in 1841 by Charles Goodyear of America.

141. Safety razor was invented by King C. Gilletle in 1895 in the USA.

142. Neon lamp was invented by Georges Claude of France in 1910.

143. Gramphone was invented by Thomas Alva Edison of America in 1878.

144. Fountain pen was invented by Lewis E. Waterman of the USA in 1884.

145. Cinema was invented by Nicolas and Jean Lumiere of France in 1895.

146. Barometer was invented by Evangelista Torricelli of Italy in 1644.

147. Ballastic missile was invented in 1944 by Wernher von Braun of Germany.

148. Celluloid was discovered in 1861 by Alexander Parke of Britain.

149. Digital computer was invented by the Harward University in 1944.

150. Electric welding was invented by Elisha Thomson in 1877.

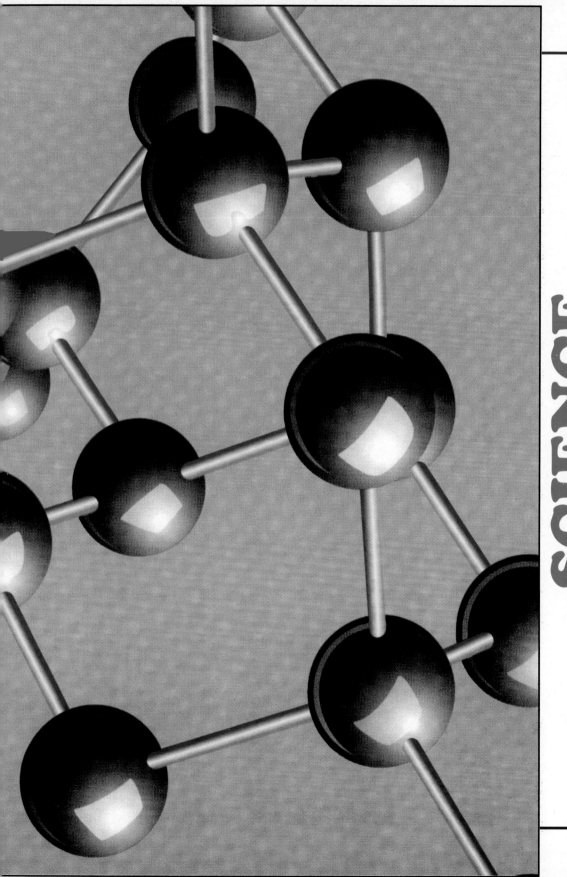

SCIENCE

Chapter 9

SCIENCE

1. Which branch of science deals with matter and other related things?
2. What is the theory that the great scientist Einstein expounded?
3. What are the two classes of matter?
4. What proves that even in atom there is a lot of space?
5. What determines the kind of an atom?
6. What is an element?
7. What holds together the protons and electrons?
8. What is a molecule?
9. What is a bond?
10. How long does a molecule of water measure?
11. What determines the weight of a molecule?
12. What is Hook's law?
13. What is elasticity?
14. What is weight?
15. What is Moh's Hardness Scale?
16. What is a crystal?
17. What is a crystalline?

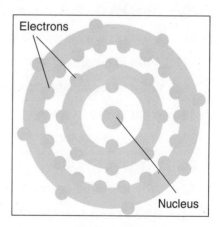

Electrons

Nucleus

BOHR'S ATOM

SULPHUR CRYSTALS

18. Who for the first time showed that crystals fall into six geometrical shapes and groups?

19. What is an alloy?

20. Bronze is an alloy. What metals mix together to make this alloy?

21. Matter usually exists in three states—solid, liquid and gas. What is the fourth state of matter.

22. What is speed?

23. What is velocity?

24. What is Doppler's Effect?

25. What is the standard unit of magnetic flux?

26. Why is heavy water used in a nuclear reactor?

27. What is chemical energy?

28. What is dynamics?

29. What is Newton's first law?

30. What is Newton's second law?

NEWTON

31. What is Newton's third law?

32. What is a catalyst?

33. What is a catalytic converter?

34. What is electrolysis?

35. What is recycling?

36. What are plastics?

37. Why are plastics harmful?

38. What is vulcanization?

39. What are the different kinds of elements?

40. What are the three states in which an element can be found?

41. What is a compound?

42. What is an atomic number?

43. On which two things does the strength of gravity depend?

44. Why is the gravity of the Earth more than that of the Moon?

45. Why do astronauts become weightless in space?

46. Who discovered the laws of gravitation?

47. Which matter has a positive charge and which matter a negative charge? When is matter electrically neutral?

48. Who discovered that an electric current created a magnetic field?

49. What is resistance?

50. Who made the first battery?

51. Who is known as the father of electric motor and electric generator?

52. What is a voltage?

53. How does a solar cell converts sunlight into electrical energy?

54. What are insulators?

55. What are conductors?

56. What makes copper a good conductor of electricity?

57. What is electricity?

58. What is galvanometer?

59. What are gamma rays?

60. What causes friction in solid objects?

61. How can friction be reduced?

62. What happens when brakes are applied in a running vehicle?

BALL BEARING IN THE ROLLER SKATES REDUCE THE FRICTION WITHOUT LUBRICANTS

63. What is air friction?

64. What is energy?

65. What is the law called under which energy cannot be created or destroyed?

66. Why do we feel warm after a brisk walk or jogging?

67. What is potential energy?

68. What is kinetic energy?

69. What is heat?

70. How things happen and work is done?

71. How much surface of the earth is covered by water?

72. What is water?

73. At what temperature does water change into gas?

74. What is Archimede's principle?

A HYDRO-ELECTRIC POWER STATION

75. What is water-cycle?

76. What is sound?

77. Why sound waves move faster through solids and liquids than the air?

78. Why do we see the flash of lightning before hearing the crash of thunder?

79. What is frequency?

80. What is an ultrasonic sound?

81. What is an oscilloscope?

82. What is the sound barrier?

83. Which aeroplane can fly at twice the speed of sound?

84. What is a sonic boom or bang?

85. When did the first supersonic flight take place?

86. What is an echo?

87. What is echo-sounding?

88. What is chemistry?

89. Who were alchemists?

90. Who discovered the relation between oxygen and the process of burning?

91. What did John Dalton discover?

92. What does biochemistry deal with?

93. What makes things visible to our eyes?

94. Why can owls and cats see at night?

95. Why does the Sun emit so much light?

96. What is the speed of light?

97. How much time does sunlight take to reach us?

98. What is a translucent object?

99. Why does light form a shadow?

100. What type of an eye does a bee have?

101. What is condensation?

MIRAGE - A SUPERSONIC AIRCRAFT

ROBERT BOYLE— AN ALCHEMIST

SUNLIGHT MAKING A SHADOW

102. What is rusting?

103. What is the result of the corrosion of aluminium?

104. What is hard water?

105. How detergents help water in removing dirt?

106. Light or electromagnetic radiation can be seen in what two forms?

107. What produces the sensation of white light of the Sun?

108. What is the visible spectrum?

109. What are the primary colours of light?

110. What are secondary colours?

111. Who first discovered that sunlight is a mixture of seven colours?

112. What are the colours of the continuous spectrum?

113. What are the primary colours of paints?

114. Why does the sky look blue?

115. What do the cone cells in our eyes do?

116. Why can we see our perfect image in the mirror?

117. Why does a swimming pool sometimes look shallower than it actually is?

118. How is a laser beam different from conventional light?

119. Who made the first laser?

120. What is the use of lasers in medicine?

121. What are some of the other uses of lasers?

122. With reference to what is time measured?

123. What is the speed of the rotation of the Earth?

124. How much distance does the Earth cover in making one round of the Sun?

125. What is a meridian?

126. When were mechanical clocks developed?

127. What is an atomic clock?

128. Who first invented rockets?

129. When and where was gunpowder invented?

130. Who in India used rockets in early 19th century?

ROCKET OF
US
AIRFORCE

131. Who developed the idea of a multistage rocket?

132. Why are sometimes extra rockets attached to the first stage?

133. What is a natural satellite?

134. What are artificial satellites?

135. For what purposes are the satellites launched?

136. When and by whom was the first satellite launched?

137. Why doesn't an artificial satellite fall on the Earth?

138. At what speed does a satellite have to travel to escape the Earth's gravitation?

139. What is the difference between a rocket and a space shuttle?

140. When was first space shuttle launched?

141. What are the three main parts of a space shuttle?

142. Which are the two space stations so far launched and used for space exploration?

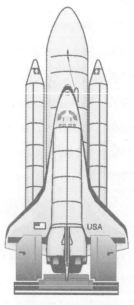

US SPACE SHUTTLE

143. What are some of the major problems being faced by astronauts?

144. What is a space suit?

145. What tasks are an astronaut required to perform in space?

146. Which spacecraft was used to launch the first ever space station Salyut-1 of Russia in 1971?

147. Why is the computer called a data processing machine?

148. What are non-computing work being done by a computer?

149. Who began the use of abacus?

150. Where was the first practical and automatic computer developed?

151. Who developed the basic design for modern computers?

152. What revolutionised the development and production of computers?

153. What is Internet?

154. Who first called the Internet as the information super highway?

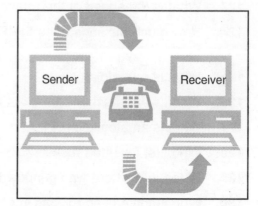

Sender   Receiver

THIS IS HOW THE INTERNET WORKS

155. When was World Wide Web (WWW) developed?

156. What is backup?

157. What is compact Disk-Read only Memory?

158. What is cursor?

159. What is the desktop?

160. What is a dialogue box?

161. What is a mouse?

162. What is megabyte?

163. What is memory?

164. What is multimedia?

165. What is an icon?

166. What is a kilobyte?

167. What does byte signify?

168. What is gigabyte (GB)?

169. What is password?

170. What is RAM?

171. What is Zoom?

172. What is software?

HARD DISK : THE PERMANENT MEMORY IN THE COMPUTER WHERE THE DATA AND PROGRAMS ARE STORED

NSWERS

1. Physics is the branch of science that studies matter and other related things.

2. Einstein expounded the Theory of Relativity. He showed that time and space can not be absolute. He was also involved in the development of Quantum Physics.

3. The two classes of matter are organics and inorganics. Animals, birds, human beings, trees, plants, vegetables, coal, leather, cotton etc. come under

ALBERT EINSTEIN

organic matter as they belong to the class of living things. Stone, iron, gold, glass, water, oil etc. come under inorganic matter as they are non-living things and never belonged to the class of living things.

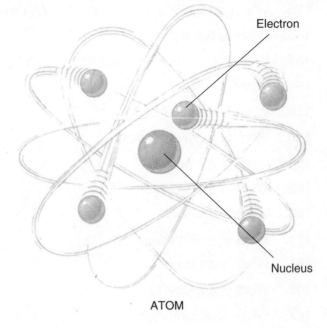

Electron

Nucleus

ATOM

4. In an atom electrons spin round the nucleus. It proves that even in atom there is much space.

5. The number of protons in an atom determines the kind of an atom. So far 105 kinds of atoms have been discovered.

6. An element is a matter made up of only one kind of atom. Iron, gold, oxygen, hydrogen are some of the 105 elements. An atom of iron has 26 protons and gold 79 protons.

7. A strong bond called ionic bonding holds the protons and electrons together in an atom.

8. A molecule is made up of atoms. It is the smallest particle of a substance. A molecule may be very simple or very complex made up of thousands of atoms arranged in a complicated pattern. A molecule of a hydrogen gas is simple one, while that of pure natural rubber is complex.

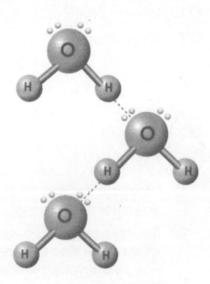

9. A bond is a strong force which is generated by electrons in an atom. For example, in a molecule of water, the negatively-charged electrons of the hydrogen atom are pulled by the positively-charged nucleus of the oxygen atom.

10. A molecule of water will measure a few billionths of an inch.

11. The weight of a molecule depends on the number of protons and neutrons in the nucleus of the atom.

WATER MOLECULES

12. Hook's law explains that the extension of a material is directly proportional to the force applied.

13. Elasticity is the property of a substance due to which it returns to its original shape and size when the deforming force is removed. For example, a rubber band can be stretched to double or more of its size. It then returns to its original size and length when that external force is removed.

14. The force with which a planet attracts an object is weight. Weight is measured in newtons (N). An object with a mass of 1kg on the Earth is about 9.8N.

15. Moh's Hardness scale is a scale from one to ten named after Friedrich Mohs (1773-1839). Diamond is the hardest at ten and talc the softest at 1. A hard object will scratch a softer object and will itself be scratched by a harder object.

16. A crystal is a substance in which the constituents are arranged in a definite geomerical form. Many crystals that appear irregularly shaped to a naked eye can be found with powerful microscope to be masses of geometrically and regularly arranged crystals.

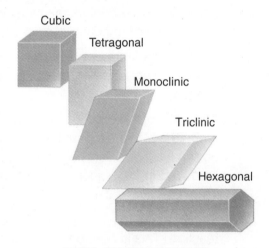

BASIC CRYSTAL SHAPES

17. A crystalline is a solid substance with a crystal structure, a regular internal arrangement of atoms, ions or molecules.

18. It was Abbe Rene Hauy who for the first time showed that crystals fall into 6 geometrical shapes and groups.

19. Alloy is a mixture of two or more metals or metal and non-metals. Bronze and brass are good examples of alloys of two metals. Steel is an alloy of a metal and a non-metal. It is a mixture of iron and carbon.

20. Bronze is an alloy. It is the result of the mixture of copper and tin.

21. The fourth state of matter is plasma; an assembly of ions and electrons. Plasma is a completely ionized gas at extremely high temperatures composed of positively charged nuclei and negative electrons.

22. The speed of an object is the distance it covers in one second. Second is a unit of time.

23. Velocity is the distance covered by an object per second in a given direction. It is a vector quantity and its units are metre/second. An object that does not change its velocity is said to possess constant velocity.

24. When the source and observer move apart, an apparent change in the frequency of a wavelength takes place. It is called Doppler's Effect.

25. Weber (Wb) is the standard unit of magnetic flux. One weber is equal to the magnetic flux linked with a circuit of one turn which when reduced to zero in one second produces an e.m.f. of one volt.

26. In heavy water, hydrogen is replaced by deuterium. It is basically used in a nuclear reacter to slow down fast neutron.

27. Chemical energy is released during a chemical reaction. It is a stored energy. Coal and petrol contain chemical energy and produce heat when burnt.

28. Dynamics is a branch of mechanics which deals with the study of behaviour of the bodies under the action of forces which change their motion.

29. A body continues to be in its state of rest or of uniform motion when the forces acting on it are equal and opposite. This is Newlon's first law.

30. The rate of change of velocity of an object is proportional to the external force acting on it. When an external force acts on an object, the acceleration produced in the object is proportional to the force. This is Newton's second law.

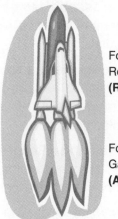

Force on Rocket **(REACTION)**

Force on Gases **(ACTION)**

NEWTON'S THIRD LAW OF MOTION

31. For every action there is an equal and opposite reaction. This is Newton's third law.

32. A catalyst is a substance that accelerates the rate of reaction but remains itself unchanged at the end of the process.

33. A catalytic converter is a device fitted in cars which converts harmful carbon monoxide, nitrogen oxide and unburnt hydrocarbons into carbon-dioxide, water and nitrogen. This device can work only with lead-free petrol.

34. Electrolysis is a process under which a chemical reaction takes place as a consequence of an electric current being passed through electrolyte. An electrolyte can be liquid, solution or paste having ions that conduct electric current. When an atom gains or loses electrons it is electrically charged and then it is known as an ion.

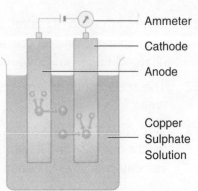

Ammeter
Cathode
Anode
Copper Sulphate Solution

ELECTROLYSIS

35. Certain materials like iron, plastic, paper, glass, aluminium etc. can be reused after the first use. This second use is called recycling. For example, waste paper is collected and recycled to produce many kinds of paper-products.

36. Plastics are synthetic polymers. Plastic articles are very popular these days as they are non-corrosive and good insulators. Plastics can be easily moulded into various designs and shapes.

37. Plastics are harmful because they are not environment-friendly. They are non-biodegradable and cannot be destroyed naturally. When burnt they produce toxic fumes, Moreover, plastic-rubbish emit methane gas which is explosive. Such rubbish gives rise to a toxic slime when rain water seeps through it. This slime pollutes ground water.

38. Vulcanization is a process to make natural raw rubber hard, tough and less temperature sensitive. In this process raw, natural rubber is heated with sulpher.

39. There are 105 kinds of different elements. As there are 105 kinds of atoms so are the number of various types of elements.

40. Solid, liquid and gas are the three states in which an element can be found. In a solid element the molecules are held together by strong bonds. Heat can change an element or substance into liquid and more heat into a vapour.

41. When two or more elements combine together in a definite proportion they make up a compound. In compounds the elements are found together in units called molecules.

42. Each element has its atomic number based on the number of protons its atom has. For example, an atom of hydrogen gas has one proton and so its atomic number is one.

43. The strength of gravity depends on the mass of a thing and the distance from one another. The more massive an object is, the greater the gravity. Small and light objects have little gravity.

44. The gravity of the Earth is more than that of the Moon because the earth has far more matter than that of the Moon. Things fall faster on the Earth than they do on the Moon.

45. Astronauts become weightless in space because then they are far away from the Earth's gravitational pull. There is no pull on them either of the Earth or any other heavenly body. It is gravity which is responsible for weight.

AN ASTRONAUT IN SPACE

46. The great scientist Sir Isaac Newton discovered the gravitational pull between various heavenly bodies. His discovery is known as Newton's laws.

47. A matter with excess of protons has an overall positive charge. And a matter with excess of electrons has an overall negative charge. A matter having equal number of protons and electrons is electrically neutral.

48. A Danish scientist Hans Oersted discovered in 1819 that an electric current created a magnetic field.

49. The resistance of a material is the power that opposes the flow of the electric current. It is the extent to which it opposes the flow of the electric current.

50. Volta made the first battery in 1800. This discovery led to many other important discoveries in the field.

51. Michael Faraday is known as the father of electric motor and electric generator.

52. A voltage is an electromotive force of supply of electricity which is measured in volts.

MICHAEL FARADAY

53. A solar cell converts the energy of sunlight into electrical energy using layers of semi-conductors.

54. A metal like polythene or acetate that does not allow electric charge to flow through it is an insulator.

55. Metals which allow free flow of electric charge through them are conductors.

56. Copper is a metal which has some electrons that are free to move through the material. These free electrons make copper a good conductor of electricity.

57. Electricity is one of the forms of energy which can be changed into different kinds of energy—heat, light, mechanical energy etc.

58. A galvanometer is an instrument for detecting small electric currents, usually of the order of 10^{-6} amp. It has a moving coil which turns when electric current flows through it. It also has a pointer across a scale that indicates the size of the current.

59. Gamma rays are emitted during decay of radioactive nuclei and when a nuclei in an excited state makes a transition to ground state or a lower energy state. It is electromagnetic radiation of very short wavelength.

60. Friction arises in solid objects because of the unevenness of the surface that are in contact. The more the unevenness, the greater the friction.

61. Friction can be reduced mainly by lubrication and by using rollers. Lubricants keep the two surfaces apart and allows them to move easily and smoothly past each other. Friction allows the rollers to grip the surface that causes the rollers to roll and so there is much less friction.

62. When brakes are used in a running vehicle the speed is reduced and the kinetic energy is converted into heat.

63. Air friction is a kind of resistance that happens when an object moves through the air. The greater the speed of the object, the more the resistance of the air.

64. Energy is the capacity of doing work. Something that makes something else work is energy.

65. Energy cannot be created or destroyed. This is because of the Laws of Conservation of Energy. Energy is always the same. You can neither subtract nor add any amount to it. It means the total amount of energy after any use or change is always exactly the same. Energy simply changes forms.

66. We feel warm after a brisk walk or jogging because our energy is then changed into heat.

67. Potential energy is a kind of energy that has been stored up and ready for use. Petrol, oil, coal, wood, food, etc. are all examples of stored up potential energy which is ready for use.

68. Kinetic energy is that energy which arises out of weight of a moving body and its speed. It is also called mechanical energy. For example, inside an electric motor, electrical energy is converted into kinetic energy because of its movement and motion. The amount of kinetic energy gained is equal to the potential energy lost.

69. Heat is a form of energy. It is the energy of constant motion of atoms and molecules in objects. In other words, heat is energy of atoms and molecules moving. The faster they move, the hotter it gets.

SUN—A SOURCE OF HEAT

70. Things happen and work is done because energy flows from one object of high temperature to another object of low temperature. In a steam engine the flow of heat energy from hot to cold areas drives the engine. This is known as heat transfer. Temperature shows how fast the molecules and atoms are moving. By heating we make the molecules to move faster.

71. Over 70 per cent of the Earth is covered by water. Three-quarters of the human body is also water.

72. Water is a compound made up of 2 atoms of hydrogen and 1 atom of oxygen per molecule. But it does not have any of the properties of either of the elements, that is, oxygen or hydrogen. The chemical formula of water is H_2O.

73. Water changes into its gaseous form at 100°C. In this form it becomes almost invisible.

74. Archimedes, a Greek mathematician, discovered that an object weighs less in water than in air. He found that the upward thrust of water exerted upon a thing immersed in water is equal to the weight of the water displaced. This is known as the Archimede's principle.

75. The natural circulation of water through the atmosphere is called water-cycle. Water is lost from the surface of the Earth both by evaporation from sea, lakes, rivers etc. and through the transpiration of plants and vegetation. The atmospheric water forms clouds, which condense to fall on the land and sea as rain or snow.

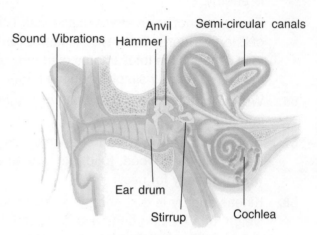

ANATOMY OF EAR

76. Sound is a sensation received by the ears. It arises out of a vibrating source. Vibrations are forward and backward movements of an object.

77. Sound waves move faster through solids and liquids because their atoms and molecules are more closely packed than that of air.

78. Light travels much faster than sound. It travels the fastest. In three seconds light travels about a million km, while sound travels just one km in 3 seconds. That is why we see the flash of lightning before hearing the crash of thunder.

LIGHTNING

79. The number of times an object vibrates in one second is called its frequency. The frequency of sound is measured in a unit called hertz.

80. A sound with frequency of over 20,000 Hz is called ultrasonic sound.

81. An oscilloscope is a device on which pictures of sound waves can be obtained.

82. The sound barrier is the increased resistance of the air to the passage of an aeroplane when it achieves the speed of sound, that is, 1200 km per hour.

83. A plane like Concorde can fly at twice the speed of sound. At such a speed the plane is said to have broken the sound barrier.

84. When an aeroplane crosses the sound barrier, it makes an explosive sound wave and it is called sonic boom or bang. It follows the plane and the vibrations are so powerful that they can break the window-panes below on the ground.

85. The first supersonic flight took place in 1947.

86. When a loud sound wave bounces back after striking a nearby hard surface, it produces an echo. When sound waves strike some hard surface, they bounce back like the rays of light are reflected by a mirror or a very smooth surface.

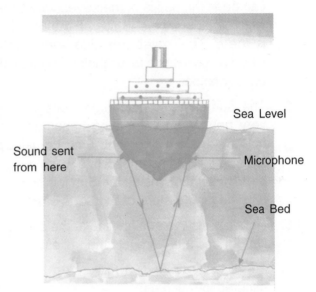

Sea Level

Sound sent from here

Microphone

Sea Bed

87. Echo-sounding is used in detecting submarines, wrecked ships, the depth of the sea, shoals of fish in deep sea, etc. A sound is sent out from the bottom of the ship. The sound waves strike the bottom of the

THE USE OF ECHO OF SOUND TO MEASURE THE DEPTH OF SEAS

water or any other object in the deep sea and then bounce back to the surface of the sea. The depth of the sea or any other object can be worked out on the basis of the time the sound waves take to travel back.

88. Chemistry is that branch of science which studies the composition of substances and their effects on one another.

89. Alchemists were the predecessors of the modern chemists. In ancient times they worked hard to discover and develop the philosopher's stone which they believed would change base metal into gold. They also wanted to search out an elixir that would prolong human life to a great extent.

JOSEPH PRIESTLEY— AN ALCHEMIST

90. Antonie Lavoisier discovered the relation between oxygen and the process of burning.

91. John Dalton discovered that atoms in the elements are joined together in definite ratios to form molecules.

92. Biochemistry deals with the substances found in living organisms including the chemical reactions occurring in such systems.

93. It is light that makes things visible to our eyes. Both light and eyes are important in seeing. In darkness it is difficult to see things.

94. Owls and cats can see at night because they can open the pupils of their eyes very wide, which enables them to use all the light that is there. Their eyes are also very elastic which helps them to focus their eyes instantly on any object.

OWL'S EYES—PUPILS WIDE OPEN

95. The Sun emits so much light because it is very hot. When something becomes very hot, it starts emitting light. First the light is red and then it becomes white when a thing becomes hotter. Inside the Sun it is so hot that the temperature is about 15 million °C. The temperature of the parts of the Sun we see is about 6000°C.

96. Light travels in a straight line at the speed of 186,281 miles per second or 299,792 km per second. It travels the fastest.

97. The Sun is about 150 million km away from us and so sunlight takes about 8 minutes to reach us.

98. A translucent object is that which allows only some light to pass through. For example, a frosted glass is a translucent object.

99. When the rays of light fall on an opaque object, they cannot pass through it and can only get past each side of it. Therefore, it forms a shadow.

100. The bee has a compound eye made up of about 5,000 tiny lenses and each lens forming a separate image. These images are combined into a whole one picture by its brain. In contrast our eye is simple.

101. Condensation is the change of a substance from gas to liquid because of cooling. For example water vapour in the atmosphere condenses into liquid when cooled.

102. Corrosion of metals is called rusting. It is a reaction of metal when it comes in contact with water and oxygen in the air. Iron gets rusted when it is exposed to water and air. Corrosion and rusting of iron can be prevented by various means, such as painting, greasing, chromium plating etc.

103. When aluminium is exposed to air and water, it starts reacting and the result is production of aluminium oxide, Aluminium oxide forms a tough layer on the surface of the metal which prevents further corrosion.

104. When water has a lot of magnesium salts and calcium, it is called hard water. It does not produce lather as its calcium forms an insoluble solid substance called scum by reacting to the soap.

105. Detergents help water in removing dirt easily by lowering the water's surface tension and consequently grease molecules are easily dissolved in water. Moreover, detergents keep the removed dirt in suspension in water.

106. Light or electromagnetic radiation can be seen as both a wave motion and or as a stream of particles called photons. In some cases light behaves as a wave and in some others as particles.

107. Different radiations have different wavelengths called the electromagnetic spectrum. When all the wavelengths of light of the Sun are perceived together, they produce the sensation of white light.

108. The white light of the Sun is a mixture of seven colours of the rainbow. These colours make up what is known as the visible spectrum. These different colours represent different wavelengths.

109. The white light of the Sun is made up of three primary colours—red, blue and green. They cannot be made from any other colours. With their combination many other colours can be obtained. Human eyes respond to these primary colours and we see and recognize all other colours by how much red, blue and green they have.

110. All other colours except red, blue and green are called secondary colours and they can be obtained by mixing primary colours together.

111. It was the British scientist Isaac Newton who for the first time discovered that white sunlight is really a mixture of seven colours of the rainbow. He passed sunlight through a prism and saw a beautiful spectrum.

112. The seven colours of the continuous spectrum are red, orange, yellow, green, blue, indigo and violet.

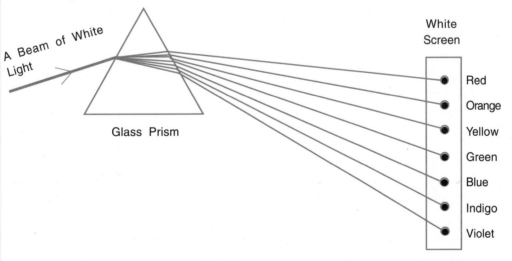

WHITE LIGHT SPLITS INTO 7 COLOURS

113. The primary colours of paints are red, yellow and blue.

114. The sky looks blue because it reflects the blue colour of the light and absorbs all other colours of the spectrum. Things look of the colour they reflect. Which colours are reflected and which are absorbed depend on the pigment of the object.

115. The cone cells in our eyes are very sensitive to colour and different wavelengths and that help us to see different colours.

116. A mirror has a very smooth and polished surface and all the rays of light that fall on it are bounced off and reflected back in exactly the same way as they arrive. And so we can see our perfect image in the mirror. In still water also the rays of light bounce off the water-surface in exactly the same pattern as they arrive.

117. Because of refraction of light sometimes a swimming pool looks shallower than it actually is. When the rays of light enter the water, they slow down and are bent. It is because of this reason that a stick immersed in water looks broken or bent.

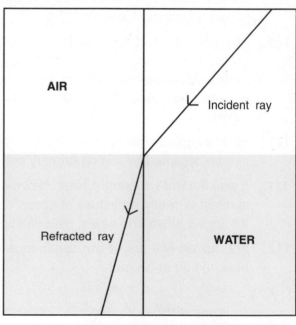

REFRACTION OF LIGHT

118. A laser beam is totally different from conventional light as it does not spread and is pencil thin. It is also so intense that it can make a hole through steel in less than a second. Being so straight, directional, narrow and intensive it can be precisely aimed even at an object on the moon. Laser beams can travel very long distances through space without spreading or growing weak.

119. A US scientist Theodore H. Maiman made the first laser in June 1960.

120. Lasers have proved very useful in the field of medicine. They are used to cut and seal tissues with such precision as not to harm the adjoining tissues. They can be focussed with such a precision during surgery that they can cut and seal tiny blood vessels and nerve endings without causing much pain and bleeding.

121. Lasers can be used in many different ways. In defence they can be used as range-finders, target seekers for pinpoint dropping of bombs, etc. They are also used to make holograms which are special photographs which give a three-dimensional image.

122. Time is measured with reference to the Earth's motion. The rotation of the Earth on its axis makes a day and its revolution round the Sun makes a year. These rotation and revolution give us our days, months, seasons and years. But minutes and seconds are measured by clock.

123. The Earth travels on its axis from east to west at a speed of 1,600 km/h and gives us the day of 24 hours.

124. The Earth covers 940 million km in making a round of the Sun in 365 days 6 hours.

125. A meridian is an imaginary line that passes through the poles. Places on the same meridian have the identical solar time. The world has been divided into 24 meridians.

126. Mechanical clocks that rang a bell were invented in Europe during the Middle Ages. These clocks were mainly used by monks in monasteries and churches to know the hours of prayers.

127. An atomic clock is accurate to one second in hundred thousand years because in it the time scale is derived from the vibrations of atoms or molecules.

128. The Chinese invented rockets about 750 years ago. They used them to repel the invasion of Mongols.

129. The Chinese invented the gunpowder some 900 years ago.

130. In early 19th century Tipu Sultan of Mysore used rockets in battles against the British armies.

131. A Russian school teacher named Konstantin Triolkovsky had the idea of using a multistage rocket in 1903.

KONSTANTIN TSIOLKOVSKY

132. Sometimes extra rockets are attached at the side of the first stage to give additional thrust at the launch.

133. A moon that revolves round a planet is its natural satellite. The Moon is the Earth's natural satellite. Mars has two moons or natural satellites called Phobos and Deimos. In other words a satellite is a small body that orbits a larger heavenly body.

134. Artificial satellites are those launched from the Earth. They are sent into space and their orbits by rockets. They revolve round the earth in their orbits.

135. Artificial satellites are launched for scientific purposes, weather forecasting, communication, spying, military purposes, etc.

SPUTNIK-2

SPUTNIK-3

ARTIFICIAL SATELLITES

136. Sputnik-1, the first unmanned satellite was launched by the erstwhile Soviet Russia in 1957. It marked the beginning of the space age and exploration.

137. An artificial satellite remains in space and its orbit because of its speed and distance from gravitational pull of the Earth. At a height of 35,900 km a satellite in orbit has to maintain a speed of 111,000 km/h. It will take the satellite 23 hours and 56 minutes to travel once round the Earth.

138. A satellite has to travel at a speed of 40,000 km/h to escape the Earth's gravitation.

139. Launch vehicles like rockets can be used only once. But a space shuttle is a reusable space vehicle. It is like an aeroplane which makes repeated journeys between its base on the Earth and the space.

140. The first space shuttle Columbia was launched on 12 April, 1981 from Kennedy Space Centre, Florida, USA. After 7 months it once again took off and went into orbit round the Earth.

141. The three main parts of the space shuttle are the orbiter, the rocket boosters and the external fuel tank. The orbiter is a winged craft that carries the astronauts, cargo, satellites, etc. From the upper deck of the orbiter, the astronauts operate the spacecraft. The 2-rocket boosters blast off the space shuttle. The external fuel tank is discarded after the space shuttle has climbed into its orbit. After its mission is complete, the orbiter re-enters the Earth's atmosphere and lands safely on a special runway.

142. The two space stations include the Russian Mir and the American Skylab. Because of the space shuttles like Challenger, Discovery and Atlantis these space stations could be visited and revisited.

143. Astronauts have to face many problems in space including weightlessness and problems of eating, drinking and breathing. In a weightless condition, the astronauts have to live in a strange world. They have to get used to weightlessness before being sent into space. They have to squeeze food and drinks into their mouth from tubes in the space. A suitable atmosphere is created in the spacecraft for their breathing.

YURI GAGARIN—THE FIRST ASTRONAUT TO GO INTO SPACE

144. Space suits are specially designed and prepared for astronauts. A spacesuit protects the astronauts from solar radiation, from tiny meteorites and keeps him warm and comfortable. It also supplies oxygen to an astronaut. It also maintains the desired pressure inside. A spacesuit is connected to the spaceship's life support system. Without such a protective spacesuit the astronaut's blood would start boiling due to low pressure of space.

145. Besides the normal and routine activities an astronaut may be required to perform many special tasks. These include retrieval of malfunctioning satellites, repairing a space station, launching of satellites from low earth orbiting platforms and going to another orbiting spaceship, work and live there for some time and then return to the mothership.

146. The Russian Salyut-1 was the first space station to be put into orbit in 1971. It was carried to and from by the Soyuz spacecraft.

SOYUZ

147. The computer is also called a data processing machine because it stores information and data and processes them according to a set of instructions called a program. It is an electronic machine capable of doing very fast calculation work with hundred per cent accuracy.

148. Today more than 80 per cent of the work done by computers is non-computational. These include traffic control, running of trains, imaging in surgery and medicine, weather forecasting, ticketing and reservation, banking, printing, satellite launching, management, education, communication, etc. The list is actually endless. Computers control and operate robots and other very complicated devices.

149. The Chinese began the use of the abacus for rapid calculations in arithmetic. They still use it and very effectively.

150. The first automatic computer that really worked was developed in 1944 at Harvard University and was called Mark-I. Then it was called a marvellous machine.

151. In the 1940s an American mathematician John Von Neumann developed the basic design for modern computers.

152. The development of microchips revolutionised the development and production of computers. It marked the beginning of a revolution and the Computer Age.

153. The Internet is a network of networks. A computer network connects countless computers with one another. Internet is a global linking of tens of thousands of businesses, institutions, universities, research organisations, advertising agencies etc. If you are hooked on the Internet, you have access to anything anywhere in the world.

154. The US Vice President Al Gore first called the Internet as the information super highway and now it is in common use among the computing fraternity.

155. The World Wide Web or W-3 was originally developed in early 1990s at the European Centre for Nuclear Research (ENCR), Geneva, Switzerland to help scientists to share their information.

156. Backup is a process of creating additional copies of data, documents and files to protect them from unexpected computer disaster. This duplication is a good standby.

157. Compact Disk-Read only Memory (CD-ROM) is a means of data storage using optical storage technology. A single CD-ROM can hold more than 650MB of information, that is one-half billion characters of text.

158. It is usually a blinking horizontal or vertical bar that moves on the computer screen and shows the position where the text or codes will be inserted or deleted.

159. The desk top is the main area of the Windows where one can open and operate programmes and files.

160. A dialogue box in the computer screen is a box that opens, lets us select, or displays messages, instructions and warnings.

161. The mouse is a small hand-held computer device, connected to the monitor. It is moved on the surface of a pad causing the cursor to move to a desired point on the screen. It is also used to enter commands.

162. A megabyte (MB) means one million bytes, or 1,024 kilobytes (1,048,576 bytes) of information or storage capacity.

8 bits =	1 Byte
1024 Bytes =	1 Kilo Byte
1024 Kilo Bytes =	1 Mega Byte
1024 Mega Bytes=	1 Giga Byte

163. Memory refers to storage capacity in the computer in binary code. The information and instructions are stored temporarily in memory.

164. A multimedia computer combines standard computer capabilities with other media as video and audio.

165. An icon is a tiny graphic image that represents an application, command or a tool. To activate it, it is clicked or double clicked.

166. Kilobyte (KB) means 1,024 bytes of information storage capacity.

167. A byte is made up of 8 bits. It is a group of eight binary digits used to represent one unit of data in the computer's memory. 1024 bytes are equal to one kilobyte (1 KB).

168. A gigabyte(GB) is equivalent to one billion bytes.

169. Password is a secret code that works as a key to access a programme or file. Without password one cannot log on.

170. Random Access Memory (RAM) is the memory that is used for temporary storage of data and programmes.

171. Zoom is used to enlarge or reduce the way text is displayed on the computer screen, but it does not affect the the way the text is going to be printed.

172. Software is the programmes used in a computer system. It enables a computer system to become operational.

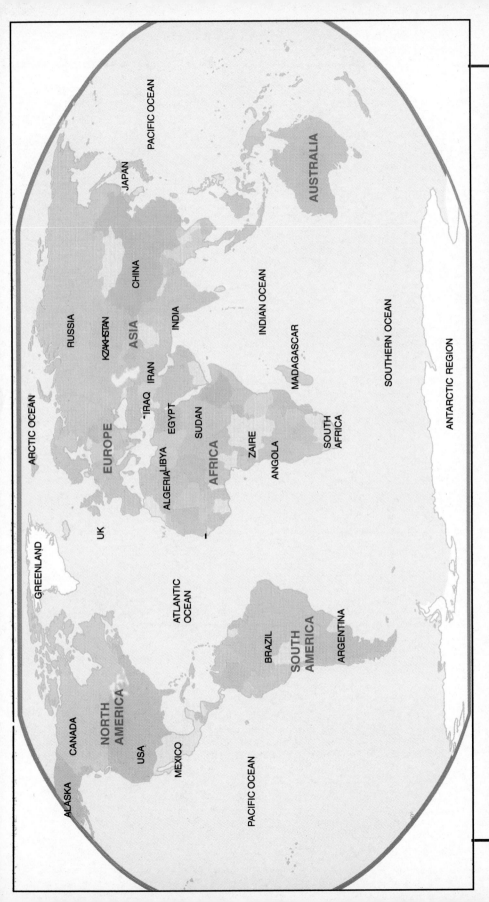

OCEANS, CONTINENTS AND COUNTRIES

Chapter 10

OCEANS, CONTINENTS & COUNTRIES

QUESTIONS

1. What was the huge continental mass that formed a single block, called some 50 million years ago?
2. Why did the Pangaea begin to break?
3. How did high mountain chains come into existence?
4. Who put forward the Theory of Continental Drift?
5. When did India break off and drift northwards from the single super continent?
6. Which is the biggest continent?
7. How were the Himalayas formed?
8. At what rate India is still moving northwards?
9. What is the maximum depth of the ocean floor?
10. With what is the ocean floor covered?
11. Where is the Thar Desert? How big is it?
12. Which is the largest desert?
13. Which is the highest waterfall?

Chapter 10

14. Which is the highest waterfall of America?

15. Which is the second highest peak after Mt. Everest?

16. Which is the highest active volcano?

17. What has been the highest temperature recorded so far. When and where was it recorded?

18. Where is kilimanjaro? What is its height?

19. How big is Antarctic circle?

20. About how many active volcanoes are there in the world?

21. What is a dormant volcano? How is it different from an extinct volcano?

22. Which has been the highest battle ground?

23. Amazon (Brazil) is the second longest river in the world after Nile (Egypt). How long is this river?

24. What would be the probable effects of an earthquake of 8-9 of Richter Scale?

25. What can be the speed of the gentle breeze?

26. Asia is the largest continent. How much percentage of total surface area of the earth it covers?

27. What is the average depth of the Indian ocean?

28. Where is Kalahari Desert located?

29. Which is the largest lake of the world?

30. Where is the lake Victoria located?

31. Which ocean has been nicknamed as the Herring Pond?

32. Which continent is called the Land of the Golden Fleece?

33. Which country is called the Cockpit of Europe?

34. What is the nickname of Mayammar (Burma)?

35. Which country is called the Land of Thousand Lakes?

WATERFALL

AMAZON RIVER

36. What is the Sorrow of China?

37. What is known as the Island of Cloves?

38. The Arabian Paninsula is the largest in the world. Which is the second largest paninsula?

39. By which nickname is Turkey called?

40. What is the nickname of New Zealand?

41. Which country is known as the Playground of Europe?

42. Which country is known as the Land of the White Elephant?

43. Which continent is called the Dark Continent?

44. What was Kampuchea formerly called?

45. What is the old name of Sri Lanka?

46. What is the capital of China, Peking now called?

47. Which country was known as Gold Coast in the past?

48. Which is the largest bay?

49. Which is the largest delta?

50. What is the highest recorded rainfall in any one year?

51. What is the highest average yearly rainfall?

52. What is the lowest recorded temperature?

53. What is the capital of Australia?

54. Which are the states that constitute the Federation of Australia?

55. Who invented the boomerang?

56. Where are penguins found?

57. What are the breeding grounds of penguins called?

58. How big is the emperor penguin?

59. Who is an Eskimo?

60. What is the house or shelter in which Eskimos live, called?

61. What is an ocean current?

62. What are the different types of ocean currents?

AN ANCIENT STATUE OF BUDDHA CARVED OUT OF A SINGLE SLAB OF GRANITE IN CENTRAL SRI LANKA

A COLONY OF EMPEROR PENGUINS

Chapter 10

63. What is oceanography?

64. Why is the coastline always changing?

65. Of what use is the study of salt contents of the sea?

66. What is a trench?

67. What is a mountain?

68. Which is the highest mountain rising above the sea floor?

69. Which mountain is the highest above the ground?

70. Which are the other very high Himalayan peaks besides Everest?

71. What is a perennial river?

72. Which is the longest river in the world?

73. Which are the Indian rivers rising in the Himalayas?

74. What is a tide?

75. Which are the major rivers of Ireland?

76. Which is the capital of Ireland?

77. Of which country does Northern Ireland form a part?

78. When was England and Scotland united?

79. Which is the longest river of France?

80. Which is the most visited monument of France?

81. Which is the highest point of the Federal Republic of Germany?

82. What caused the Second World War?

83. When were the two Germanys united?

84. What is the Midnight Sun?

85. Which are the main active volcanoes of Iceland?

86. What is the Parliament of Iceland called?

87. Why were the Danes called Vikings in ancient times?

MOUNT EVEREST

PINELOGS STACKED IN THE BORDEAUX REGION IN FRANCE

ACTIVE VOLCANO

88. Name the currency and capital of Denmark.

89. Which are the major rivers of Greece?

90. Which were the two famous city-states of ancient Greece?

91. What is the biggest industry of Greece?

92. What does Mesopotamia mean?

93. When did Iraq invade Kuwait and with what result?

94. When did Persia change its name to Iran?

95. When did the USA come into existence?

96. When did Alaska become part of the USA?

97. When did the USA emerge as a great power?

98. Which is the highest point of the USA?

99. By which river system are drained the central plains of the USA?

STATUE OF A DISCUS THROWER BY MYRON (450 BC, GREECE)

100. By whom was America (USA) discovered?

101. What Columbus felt when he first reached America?

102. Why is the USA called America?

103. When did Vasco da Gama, the Portuguese discover direct sea-route to India?

104. Which city can be called the capital of the world?

105. When were the pyramids built? What purpose did they serve?

106. When was Egypt declared a Republic?

107. Which dam in Egypt is a source of irrigation for more than a million acres of land in the southern region?

108. By what name was Afghanistan known earlier?

NATIVE AMERICAN

109. Which river forms the northern border of Afghanistan?

110. Which group or movement has emerged as a new power in Afghanistan?

111. Where is Mexico located?

112. What are the main agricultural products of Mexico?

113. What separates the Republic of Argentina from Chile?

114. When and with whom did Argentina fight the Falkland Island war?

115. Where is the Republic of Chile located?

116. When did Chile get independence?

117. Who abused and violated human rights during 1973-1988 in Chile?

118. Which are the two most mighty rivers of Brazil?

STRANGE STONE HEADS ON ESTER ISLAND IN CHILE

119. Which was the capital of Brazil before Brasilia?

120. What are the biggest agricultural produce of Brazil?

121. Which are the major rivers of Canada?

122. In how much area is Canada spread?

123. What are the main exports of Canada?

WOODEN DOLLS, TRADITIONAL RUSSIAN TOYS

124. By what is the Republic of Russia characterized?

125. What is the average annual temperature of Siberia?

126. When was St. Petersburg founded?

127. When did Lenin become the dictator and supreme ruler of Russia?

128. When was the Commonwealth of Independent States formed?

129. What separates Sicily from Italy?

130. Which are the two active volcanoes of Italy?

131. When was Italy at the centre of the great Roman Empire?

132. When was Italy declared a Republic?

133. What characterizes Spain?

THE LEANING TOWER OF PISA IN ITALY

134. When was the Spanish Armada defeated and what was its consequences?

135. What type of state is Spain?

136. What are the main industries of Spain?

137. What small but valuable things the Swiss make in a big way?

138. Which is the well known glacier of Switzerland?

139. What makes Switzerland a multilingual country?

140. In what does Switzerland specialize?

141. When can one see the Midnight Sun in Norway?

142. Which is the largest lake, the longest river and the highest mountain of the Kingdom of Norway?

143. When did Norway join NATO?

144. Which world-famous prizes are awarded in Oslo, the capital of Norway?

HOUSEBOATS IN THE CENTRE OF AMSTERDAM IN NETHERLANDS

145. What is very special about Netherlands (Holland)?

146. Which is the capital of Holland and what is its average temperature?

147. Which sector of Netherlands forms the largest industrial sector?

148. Which country is called the Land of Thunder Dragon and what is its capital?

149. Which are the main rivers of Bhutan?

150. Since when the absolute monarchy has been changed in Bhutan?

151. Which is the capital of Nepal and what is the average annual temperature there?

152. What political system now prevails in Nepal?

153. Who became the first Prime Minister of independent India?

154. When and where did Indus Valley Civilization develop in India?

155. When did India's recorded history begin?

PT. JAWAHAR LAL NEHRU

156. When did Muslim invasion of India begin and who established the Mughal Empire?

157. What is the total area covered by India?

158. On which two occasions Indo-Pakistan war broke out?

159. When did India become a Republic?

160. When and where did India conduct its nuclear tests?

161. When was the system of Apartheid adopted in South Africa?

162. When did the system of racial discrimination and segregation called Apartheid ended completely?

163. When was Nelson Mandela, the President of African National Congress finally released?

164. What are the biggest products of South Africa?

165. Which Indian city is called the city of the Golden Temple?

166. Which Indian city is called the venice of the East or the Queen of the Arabian Sea?

167. Which hills in South India are famous?

168. What does Punjab literally mean?

169. Which is main river that drains the Islamic Republic of Pakistan?

170. When did Zulfikar Ali Bhutto become Pakistan's Prime Minister? By whom was he later executed?

171. Who became the first woman Prime Minister of Pakistan?

172. Of how many islands and islets is Indonesia made up?

173. How many volcanic peaks are there in Indonesia?

BUDDHIST TEMPLE ON THE ISLAND OF JAVA (INDONESIA) HAS 72 BELL-SHAPED STRUCTURES

174. When did Indonesia become independent? Who became its President?

175. How large is China?

176. When was China declared a Republic?

177. When did China conduct its last nuclear test?

178. How is Malaysia a multiracial country?

179. What is the largest product of Malaysia?

180. What type of political system prevails in Malaysia?

181. Which are the major islands that make up Japan?

182. Which are the chief ports of Japan?

183. What type of political system prevails in Japan?

184. What made Japan to surrender during the Second World War?

185. Who is the present Emperor of Japan?

SNOW-CAPPED SLOPES OF MOUNT FIJI IN JAPAN

186. What is the great tourist attraction in Cambodia?

187. What is the capital of Cambodia?

188. Who became an instrument in the killing of millions of innocent Cambodians during 1975-78?

189. When was Bangladesh born?

190. Who became the first President of Bangladesh?

191. What causes heavy losses in Bangladesh?

192. What is the major agricultural product of Bangladesh?

193. Which country was formerly known as Rhodesia?

194. Which is the capital of Zimbabwe?

195. What is the main river of Zimbabwe?

196. Which famous fall is located in Zimbabwe?

197. Which is the third largest country of Africa?

198. A river, second only to Nile flows through Zaire. What is its name?

199. Which is the capital of Zaire?

200. What metal forms the key export of Zaire?

201. Which is the capital of Kenya?

202. What is the currency of Kenya?

JUTE FIELD—BANGLADESH'S MOST IMPORTANT EXPORT

203. What are the 2 main cash crops of Kenya?

204. Which are the 2 major rivers of Britain?

205. Of which parts does the United Kingdom of Great Britain comprise?

206. What is the population density of the UK?

207. Time was when it was said that the sun never set on it. What did it mean?

208. When were England and Scotland joined together?

209. London is the city of museums. Which museum is the largest in London?

210. What are the star attraction of the Tower of London?

211. Why is Westminster Abbey famous?

212. Why is St. Paul's Cathedral so famous?

NSWERS

1. The huge continental mass that formed a single block some 50 million years ago was called Pangaea.

2. The Pangaea began to break because of the movement to tectonic plates and so the continents moved in different directions sliding past one another.

3. The drifting apart and clashing of the tectonic plates with one another caused the folds in the earth's crust and high mountain-chains came into existence.

4. The Theory of Continental Drift was put forward by a German scientist Alfred Wegner (1880-1930).

5. About 10 million years ago India broke off and drifted northwards from the single super continent.

6. Asia is the biggest continent with 44,000,000 sq km area, the 8.6 per cent of total surface area.

7. In the beginning there were no Himalayas but a vast shallow ocean between India and Tibet. Then the land masses on either side collided with each other as a result of continental drift forcing underwater areas upwards and creating the Himalayas.

8. India is still moving northwards at the rate of 2.5 to 3 cm per year.

9. The maximum depth of the ocean floor is about 3,800 metres.

10. The ocean floor is covered with a clay called ooze. It was formed from the shells of tiny sea-creatures.

11. Thar desert is a great desert in the north-west India spreading over about 260,000 sq. km. of area.

12. Sahara Desert is the largest. It is in North Africa and covers 8,800,000 sq. km. of the land.

13. Angel Falls of Venezuela is the highest waterfall with 979 mt height.

14. Yosemite is the highest waterfall of America with 739 mt height.

SAND DUNES IN A DESERT

15. K-2 in Tibet, a Himalayan peak is the second highest peak in the world. It stands 8,611 mt high.

16. Gaulltiri of Chile is the highest active volcano of the world with 6,060 mt height.

17. The highest recorded temperature has been 58°C. It was recorded in Libya on 13th Sept. 1922.

18. Kilimanjaro mountain is in Tanzania. It is 5895 mt high.

19. Antartic circle is 13,900,000 sq. km.

20. There are about 800 active volcanoes in the world.

21. A dormant volcano remains asleep, without erupting for a long time. An extinct volcano never erupts again.

22. Siachin in India (Himalaya) has been the highest battle ground.

23. Amazon is 6,437 km long.

24. An earthquake of 8-9 intensity of Richter scale would be very devastating and destructive. There would be general panic, buildings would be destroyed and even rivers may change their course.

25. The light breeze blows at the speed of 13-20 km per hour.

26. Asia covers 8.6 per cent of total surface area and 29.3 per cent of total land area of the earth.

27. The average depth of the Indian Ocean is 3,963 mt.

28. Kalahari Desert is in Botswana (Africa).

29. Caspian Sea is regarded as the largest lake.

30. The lake Victoria is located in Tanzania-Uganda.

31. Atlantic Ocean has been nicknamed as the Herring Pond.

32. Australia is called the Land of the Golden Fleece.

33. Belgium is called the Cockpit of Europe.

34. The nickname of Burma is the land of the Golden Pagoda.

35. Finland is called the Land of Thousand Lakes.

36. The river Hwango Ho is called the Sorrow of China.

37. Madogascar is known as the Island of Cloves.

38. Southern Indian Paninsula is the second largest in the world.

39. Turkey is called by the nickname of the Sick Man of Europe.

40. New Zealand is called the Britain of the South.

41. Switzerland is known as the Playground of Europe.

42. Thailand is known as the Land of the White Elephant.

43. Africa is called the Dark Continent.

44. Kampuchea was formerly called as Cambodia.

45. The old name of Sri Lanka is Ceylon.

46. Peking is now called Beijing.

47. Ghana was known as Gold Coast in the past.

48. Hudson Bay in Canada is the largest bay.

49. Sunder Bans in India and Bangladesh is the largest delta created by Ganga and Brahmputra rivers.

50. The highest recorded rainfall in any one year is 26,461 mm at Cherapunji in India.

51. The highest average yearly rainfall is 11,455 mm in Hawaii.

52. The lowest recorded temperature is - 88.38°C at Vostok, Antarctica.

53. Canberra is the capital of Australia.

54. The Federation of Australia consists of six states : New South Wales, Victoria, Queensland, South Australia, Western Australia and Tasmania.

55. The boomerang was invented by the Aborigines of Australia who reached there thousand of years ago from South-East Asia. A boomerang is a simple weapon in

ABORIGINES IN AUSTRALIAN SUB-CONTINENT PLAY A LONG, THICK WOODEN PIPE CALLED A DIDGERIDOO

the form of a curved stick that flies in a circle and comes back to you when you throw it at a target.

56. Penguins are found in the oceans of the southern hemisphere, particularly the Antarctic region.

57. The breeding grounds of penguins are called rookeries.

58. The emperor penguin is over one metre high and some 36 kg in weight.

59. An Eskimo is a member of a race of people who live in very cold areas of North America. It is believed that they migrated from Central Asia during the last great Ice Age.

60. The shelter or house in which Eskimos live is called an igloo or iglu. Igloos are made in winter with blocks of snow and ice.

61. An ocean current is a channel of warm or cold water caused by variation of temperature of water. The difference in water temperature in oceans and seas leads to formation of currents which move from one direction to another.

IGLOO

62. There are three different types of ocean currents—stream currents, drift currents and upwelling currents.

63. Oceanography is the science and study of oceanic phenomena. It studies all subjects connected with the ocean.

64. The coastline is the region of the earth where the sea and the earth meet. It is always changing because of tides, storms and other activities of the sea and the rivers falling in it. A major rise in sea-level because of the melting of snow and ice-caps submerges large coastal areas and new coastline emerges creating big bays.

65. The study of salt contents of the sea helps us to know how old the seas might have been.

66. A trench is a long, narrow and deep, steep-sides depression in the ocean floor. There are many huge and mysterious trenches on the ocean floor. The Mariana Trench in West Pacific is one of the longest trenches measuring 2,250 km in length. It is also the deepest trench with a depth of 11,022 m.

67. A mountain is a natural elevation of the earth's surface rising to a peak. Its height is greater than that of a hill.

68. Mauna Kea, near Hawaii Islands with a height of 4,205 m above sea level and 4,877 m below the sea is the highest mountain rising above the sea floor.

69. Mount Everest with a height of 8,848 m is the highest mountain rising above the ground. It is on the border between Tibet and Nepal.

70. Besides Everest the other very high Himalayan peaks are Kanchenjunga (8,597 m), Lhotse (8,501), Makalu (8,481 m), Dhaulagiri (8,172 m), Cho-Oyu (8,153 m), Manasulu (8,125 m), Nanga Parbat (8,125 m) and Annapurna. K-2 is the second highest Himalayan peak (8,611 m).

71. A perennial river is ever flowing because it is snow-fed or it has some other ever rich source. An ephemeral river is seasonal and flows only in the rainy season.

72. River Nile in Egypt is the longest river with a length of 6,695 km.

73. The Indian rivers that rise in the Himalayas are the Ganga, Yamuna and Brahmaputra. Brahmaputra and Ganga are international rivers.

74. Tide is the alternate rising and falling of the sea-water and that of the connected rivers. Tides are caused by the gravitational pull and attraction of the Moon and the Sun.

75. Shannon, Liffey and Slaney are the major rivers of Ireland.

76. Dublin is the capital of Ireland.

77. Northern Ireland forms a part of the United Kingdom of Great Britain. The other parts are England, Scotland and Wales.

78. England and Scotland were joined together in 1801 by an Act of Parliament.

79. Loire is the longest river of France with a length of 1,020 km.

AN IRISH FOLK GROUP

80. The Eiffel Tower in Paris is the most visited monument of France.

81. Zugspitze, with a height of 2,962 m, is the highest point of Germany. It is in the Alps Mountains.

82. The German dictator Hitler's acts of aggression caused the Second World War. The War resulted in German defeat and partition of Germany into West and East Germany.

83. The two Germanys were united into one nation on October 3, 1990.

84. Because of the Earth's tilt the Sun shines all night as well as all day in some countries. Midnight sun results when there is no sunset at all for many days or weeks. This phenomenon can be seen in Iceland.

85. Hekal (1,491 m), Helgafell (215 m) and Surtsey (174 m) are the main active volcanoes of Iceland.

86. The Parliament of Iceland is called Althing.

REYKJAVIK, THE CAPITAL CITY OF ICELAND

87. The Danes were called Vikings in ancient times because they were great voyagers, daredevils, navigators and explorers. They often ravaged the coasts of Europe from 8th to 10th centuries.

88. Krone is the currency of Denmark and Copenhagen is the capital.

89. The major rivers of Greece are Nestes, Strimon and Arkthos.

90. Athens and Sparta were the two famous city-states of ancient Greece.

91. Tourism is Greece's biggest industry and source of income.

92. Mesopotamia means between the two rivers. Iraq is known as Mesopotamia because it is located between the rivers Tigris and Euphrates. Doab also means the same. The vast alluvial plains between Ganga and Yamuna in India is known by this name.

93. Iraq invaded Kuwait in August 1990 which led to the 1991 Gulf War, defeat of Iraq and imposition of sanctions against it by United Nations.

94. Iran changed its name from Persia to present one in 1925.

95. On March 4, 1759 the United States of America came into existence in the wake of the acceptance of the Federal Constitution by 9 out of the 13 states.

96. The USA purchased Alaska from Russia in 1867.

97. During the First World War the USA sided with the Allies and emerged as a great power. Again after World War II it emerged as a superpower.

BRICK MINARET OF GREAT MOSQUE OF SAMARRA IN IRAQ

Chapter 10

98. Mt. McKinley with a height of 6,194 m in Alaska is the highest point in the USA.

99. The central plains of the USA are drained by the great Red River Missouri-Mississippi system.

100. It is believed that a Spaniard named Columbus discovered America in 1492. But before him the Vikings from Scandinavia had set foot on America.

101. When Columbus first reached America he thought he had reached India. Actually he wanted to discover India. He did not realize he had discovered a new continent.

102. An Italian named Amerigo Vespucci reached South America on June 16, 1497 and claimed that he had discovered the New World. Therefore, in 1507 the name of America was first coined and used. America means Amerigo's land.

103. In 1497, the Portuguese navigator and explorer Vasco da Gama reached India via the Cape of Good Hope. Thus, he opened the direct sea-route to India by landing on the Arabian seashore.

VASCO DA GAMA

104. New York city, USA can be called the capital of the World.

105. The Pyramids were built some 4,000 years ago and served as tombs for Egyptian Pharoahs. The Pyramids are the oldest of the ancient wonders.

106. Egypt was declared a Republic in 1953.

107. Aswan Dam on Nile is a source of irrigation for more than a million acres of land in Southern Egypt.

108. Afghanistan was earlier known as Bactria or Ariana, the Land of the Rising Sun.

109. Amu Darya (Oxus) forms the Northern border of Afghanistan.

110. The Islamic and fundamentalist group called Taliban has emerged as a new power in Afghanistan.

111. The Republic of Mexico consists of narrow coastal plains, a steep plateau in the centre and the low land of the Yucatan peninsula extending into the Gulf of Mexico in the south-east.

112. The main agricultural products of Mexico are maize, rice, wheat, sugar, cotton and coffee.

MODEL CELEBRATING
MEXICO'S DAY OF THE DEAD
FIESTA

113. The Andes range separates Argentina from Chile.

114. In 1982 Argentina fought the Falkland Island war with Britain and lost.

115. The Republic of Chile is located on the western sea-coast of south America. It occupies a long strip of land between Peru and Bolivia in the north to Cape Horn in the south.

TRADITIONAL SKILLED HORSE-RIDING IN ARGENTINA

116. Chile got independence in 1818.

117. Military junta ruler Augusto Pinochet abused and violated human rights in Chile during 1973-1988.

118. Amazon and Sao Francisco are the two mighty rivers of Brazil.

119. Before Brasilia, Rio de Janeiro was the capital of Brazil. It was in 1960 that is was moved to Brasilia.

120. Brazil is the world's largest producer of coffee, banana, sugar and the second biggest producer of oranges, maize and cocoa.

121. Mackenzie in the west and St. Lawrence in the east are the main rivers of Canada.

THE KAMAYURA— NATIVE PEOPLE OF BRAZIL LIVING IN THE RAIN FORESTS

122. Canada is spread over 9,976,139 sq. km. of area.

123. Canada is the world's second largest exporter of wheat and the world's largest producer of asbestos, zinc, silver and nickel.

124. The Republic of Russia is characterized by vast plains in the west, Siberian low lands in the east and Siberian plateau in the north. Ural Mountains separate Russia from East Europe. There are thousands of lakes and

SIBERIAN HOUSES

several rivers. Rivers include Lena, Ob, Pechora, Indigirka, Amur, Volga, Ural etc. The major lakes are Caspian Sea, Taymyr and Baikal.

125. The north-east Siberia is the coldest region of Russia with an average annual temperature of –46°C in January and, 16°C in July.

126. St. Petersburg was founded and made the capital in 1703 during the reign of Peter the Great.

127. Lenin became the dictator and supreme ruler of Russia in 1917.

128. After the collapse of the USSR a new Commonwealth of Independent States (CIS) was formed in 1991.

129. The island of Sicily is separated from the mainland of Italy by the 4 km wide strait of Messina.

130. Mount Etna in Sicily and Mount Vesuvius are the two active volcanoes of Italy.

131. In the third century Italy was at the centre of the great Roman Empire.

132. In 1945 Mussolini was put to death and in 1946 Italy was declared a Republic.

133. Spain is characterized by a central plateau, mountains and Tagus, Ebro and Guadiana rivers.

134. The Spanish Armada was defeated by Britain in 1588. It marked the decline of Spain as a great colonial power.

135. Spain is a constitutional monarchy with a parliamentary system of government. The monarch is the head but the real power is vested in the Prime Minister.

136. Wine, textiles, iron, steel, ship-building electrical goods, cars, fishing, forestry and tourism are the main industries of Spain.

137. Switzerland lacks minerals and other raw material needed for heavy industry, so the Swiss make small but valuable things like watches in a big way. Watch-making is a national industry of Switzerland.

138. Aletsch is a well-known glacier of Switzerland.

CHALETS NESTLE ON THE ALPINE PASTURE IN SWITZERLAND

139. The use of French, Italian and Romasch make Switzerland a multi-lingual country.

140. Switzerland specializes in such high technology products as precision instruments, watches, drugs, chemicals, machinery and textiles.

141. One can see the Midnight Sun in Norway during the summer months of mid-May till July-end. During this period the Sun does not go down the horizon even at midnight.

142. Lake Major is the largest lake; Golomma the longest river and Galdhopiggen the highest mountain of Norway.

143. Norway joined North Atlantic Treaty Organisation (NATO) in 1949.

144. The world-famous Nobel Prizes are awarded every year in Oslo, the capital of Norway.

145. The Kingdom of Netherlands (Holland) is the only country with much of its land below sea-level. This is very special about Netherlands. It is protected by coastal dunes and artificial dykes.

146. Amsterdam is the capital of Holland. With cool, temperate maritime climate, the average temperature of Amsterdam ranges from 2 °C in January to 17 °C in July.

147. Food-processing forms the largest industrial sector of Netherlands. Holland is also one of the world's largest exporter of dairy products.

148. The Kingdom of Bhutan (Druk-Yul) is called the Land of Thunder Dragon. Thimpu is its capital.

149. Manas and Wong Chu are the main rivers of Bhutan.

150. Since 1969 absolute monarchy has been changed into constitutional monarchy in Bhutan.

TRADITIONAL FARMHOUSES IN BHUTAN

151. Kathmandu is the capital of the land-locked Himalayan Kingdom of Nepal. Its annual average temperature ranges from 0 °C in January to 24 °C in July.

152. Nepal is a constitutional monarchy with the King as the Head of State and the Prime Minister as the Head of the Government. Nepal has a multi-party democracy with a Parliament.

153. Pt. Jawaharlal Nehru was the first Prime Minister of independent India.

154. The ancient Indian civilization is known as the Indus Valley Civilization. It developed around the river Sindhu (Indus) in Harappa and Mohenjodaro about 4,000 years back.

155. The recorded history of India began with the advent of Gautam Buddha.

156. The Muslim invasion of India began in 7th century and Babar established the Mughal Empire in 1526.

157. India is the seventh largest country of the world covering an area of 32,87,263 sq. km. It measures some 3,214 km from north to south between extreme latitudes and some 2,993 km from east to west between extreme longitudes.

158. Indo-Pakistan war broke out on two occasions : first in 1965 and then again in 1971.

159. India became a Republic in 1950.

160. On 11 and 13 May, 1998 India successfully conducted nuclear tests at Pokhran in Rajasthan. India had conducted its first nuclear test at the same site in 1974.

161. The minority white regime in South Africa adopted the system of Apartheid in 1948.

162. The system of racial discrimination and segregation called Apartheid ended completely in South Africa in April 1994 when a new multi-racial Parliament was elected and then on 10th May Nelson Mandela was sworn in as the first black President.

HAWA MAHAL, JAIPUR, RAJASTHAN

163. Nelson Mandela, the President of African National Congress was finally released in 1990 after more than 27 years of imprisonment.

164. Gold and diamond are the two biggest products of South Africa. In uranium export also it is a leading country.

165. Amritser is called the City of the Golden Temple.

166. Cochin is called the Venice of the East, or the Queen of the Arabian Sea.

167. Nilgiri Hills located in South India are called the Blue Mountains.

NELSON MANDELA, WITH HIS PARTY SUPPORTERS

168. Punjab literally means the Land of Five Rivers.

169. The river Sind (Indus) drains the vast fertile plains of Pakistan before falling into the Arabian Sea near Karachi. The other rivers of Pakistan are Jhelum, Chenab and Sutlej.

170. Zulfikar Ali Bhutto became the Prime Minister of Pakistan in 1970. He was overthrown in a military coup by Gen. Zia ul-haq in 1977. He executed Bhutto in 1979.

171. Benazir Bhutto, the daughter of Zulfikar Ali Bhutto became the first woman Prime Minister of Pakistan in 1988.

172. Indonesia is made up of 13,677 islands and islets, of which about 6,000 are inhabited. Indonesia is the world's largest island group-state.

DISTINCTIVE WOODEN HOUSES WITH CURVED ROOFS IN INDONESIA

173. There are about 100 volcanic peaks in Indonesia, of which 15 are active.

174. Indonesia became independent in 1945 and Sukarno was chosen as the President.

175. In terms of population China is the largest country. It is also the third largest country in area occupying 9,561,000 sq km of land.

176. In 1949 Mao Zedong declared China the People's Republic and in 1954 a Soviet-style constitution was adopted.

177. China is a nuclear power. It conducted its last nuclear test on July 29, 1996.

A GIRL PERFORMING WUSHU, AN ANCIENT CHINESE MARTIAL ART

KITE FLYING—A POPULAR SPORT IN MALAYSIA

178. The Federation of Malaysia is a multiracial country as it comprises many racial and ethnic groups. Fifty-five per cent of its population is Malay, 33.4 per cent Chinese, 10.1 per cent Indians and 1.4 per cent others.

179. The largest product of Malaysia is natural rubber.

180. Malaysia is a constitutional monarchy. The monarch is the Head of State and the Prime Minister Head of the Government. It is Federal Parliamentary system.

181. The main islands that make up Japan (Nipon) are Honshu, Hokkaido, Kyushu and Shikoku. There are also a number of smaller islands.

182. The chief ports of Japan are Yokohama, Kobe, Nagoya and Osaka.

183. There is constitutional monarchy in Japan. The monarch is Head of the State and the Prime Minister with his cabinet, the Head of the Government. The Parliament consists of the House of Representatives and the House of Councillors.

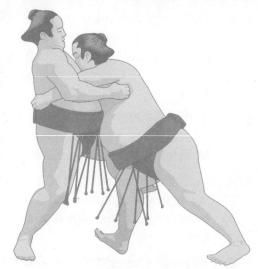

SUMO IS THE NATIONAL WRESTLING SPORT OF JAPAN

184. Japan surrendered to the allied forces because of bombing and devastation of its two cities, Hiroshima and Nagasaki.

185. At present Akihito is the Emperor of Japan. He succeeded his father after the latter's death in 1989.

186. The famous temple complex of Angkor Wat is the great tourist attraction in Cambodia. It is the largest cultural monument of the world.

TYPICAL SINGLE-STORY
RURAL HOUSES IN CAMBODIA

ANGKOR WAT

187. Phnom Penh is the capital of Cambodia.

188. Pol Pot the Khmer Rouge dictator became the instrument of killings of over 3 million innocent Cambodians during 1975-78.

189. Bangladesh was born on 16 December, 1971 following a popular rebellion and civil war against Pakistan. Then it was part of Pakistan and was called East Pakistan.

190. Sheikh Mujibur Rehman became the first President of Bangladesh but he was assassinated on 15 August, 1975 in a military coup.

191. There are frequent floods and sea-storms which cause heavy loss of men and material.

192. The major agricultural product of Bangladesh is raw jute which is about 70 per cent of the world's total jute production.

193. Zimbabwe was formerly known as Rhodesia.

194. Harare is the capital of Zimbabwe.

195. Zambezi is the chief river of Zimbabwe.

196. The famous Victoria fall is located in Zimbabwe.

197. Zaire is the third largest country on the continent of Africa.

VICTORIA FALL, ZIMBABWE

198. The river Zaire is one of the largest rivers, and the second largest after Nile in Africa flows through Zaire.

199. Kinshesha is the capital city of Zaire.

200. Copper is the key export from Zaire. Country's economy is very much dependent on this metal and its international prices.

201. Nairobi is the capital of Kenya.

202. Shilling is the currency of Kenya, which is divided into 100 cents.

203. Coffee and tea are 2 main cash crops of Kenya.

204. Severn and Thames are the 2 major river of Britain.

TWO-HORNED RHINOCEROS FOUND IN KENYA

205. The United Kingdom of Great Britain comprises of England, Scotland, Weles and Northern Irland.

206. The UK is very densely populated country. Its population density is 376 persons per sq. km.

207. Time was when Britain ruled all over the world and the sun never set on its colonies and territories.

208. England and Scotland were joined together in 1801.

209. The Victoria and Albert Museum is the largest in London.

210. Kohinoor and the star of Africa are the crown jewels. These are the two star attractions of the Tower of London.

211. West minister Abbey in London has been the place for every British Coronation since 1066. It has also been a final destination and resting place of many of Britain in aristocracy and literary figures.

212. St. Paul's cathedral has a very large dom which is one of the largest domes in the entire Christian world.

ANCIENT HISTORY

Chapter 11

ANCIENT HISTORY

QUESTIONS

1. One of which ancient civilizations of the world developed between the rivers Tigris and Euphrates?

2. Can you name 2 famous Sumerian cities?

3. Sumerians were very intelligent people. They used decimal system of number and devised a calendar. But what was their most important contribution?

4. What is cuneiform?

SUMERIAN PEOPLE MAKING MUD BRICKS

SUMERIAN FARMERS MENDING A CANAL

5. What was at the centre of the Sumerian activities?

6. With which modern state can the ancient Sumerian cities be identified?

7. How were the Sumerian civilization and cities destroyed?

8. Which king of Babylon was most famous?

EGYPTIAN TOMB PAINTING

9. Babylon was also famous for its magnificent gardens regarded as one of the seven wonders of the world. What were these gardens called?

10. In ancient Egypt, the kings were worshipped like gods. What honorary title were they given?

11. Why did an Egyptian King in ancient time marry only a sister or half-sister?

12. Egypt is famous for its ancient monuments like pyramide and sphinx at Giza built around 2600 BC. Why were these so huge structures raised?

13. What were the most important cities of ancient Egypt?

14. Why is Egypt called the 'Gift of Nile?'

15. Who ruled over Egypt during 525-404 BC?

16. Who conquered Egypt in 332 BC?

17. Who ruled over Egypt after Alexander?

18. When did Egypt become a part of the Roman Empire?

19. Who was Cleopatra?

20. What were hieroglyphics?

21. What is a mummy?

22. Why are Mohenjodaro and Harappa famous names in Indian history?

A TRADING SHIP OF INDUS VALLEY CIVILIZATION

23. Where did the Aryans settle in India in the beginning?

24. When did the Aryans come to India?

25. Which record book is the earliest source of ancient Indian culture and life?

26. What is the most important difference between Indus Valley civilization and the early Aryan civilization?

27. What helped the Aryans to conquer the non-Aryans in India in those ancient times?

INDUS VALLEY PEOPLE—OXEN BEING USED FOR PULLING CARTS

28. Which are the two famous epics of India?

29. What was the reason of fall and destruction of Indus Valley civilization?

30. Who founded the great empire of Magadha?

31. Where was Gautam Buddha born?

32. What does 'Buddha' means?

33. When did Alexander of Macedonia invade India?

34. Which Indian King put up tough resistance against Alexander?

35. Who was Chandragupta Maurya?

36. Who was Chankya?

37. What are other two well known names of Chanakya?

38. Which general of Alexander entered into matrimonial alliance with the Chandragupta Maurya? Why did he do so?

39. Who was Ashoka?

40. Why Ashoka became a Buddhist?

41. What did Ashoka do to spread Buddhism?

42. How much of Indian sub-continent did Ashoka's empire encompass?

STATUE OF THE BUDDHA'S HEAD

43. Who restored Patliputra to its former glory and splenour?

44. Under the rule of which king did Hindu India achieved the Golden Age?

45. With which Era is Chandragupta II associated? What was his popular name?

46. When did this Era begin?

47. Which great poet-dramatist lived in Chandragupta Vikrmaditya's court?

48. What was the court language of the Guptas?

49. When did the ancient Greek civilization begin?

50. What are some of the important contributions of the Greek civilization?

51. Ancient Greece consisted of many famous city states. Of these which were most famous?

52. The Greeks had many gods and goddesses. Where did they live?

53. The golden period of ancient Greek civilization was between 500 BC to 336 BC. By what famous name is this period called?

54. What for were the Spartans well-known?

STATUE OF A SPARTAN WARRIOR

55. Iliad and Odyssey are two great and world famous epics of ancient Greece. Who was their author?

56. The ancient Greek civilization is also known as Minon Civilization which grew up in Crete from 2300 BC to 1400 BC. Why is it called Minon Civilization?

57. What is Marathon?

58. Why was sport so important to Greeks?

59. Where were the Olympic Games held in Ancient Greece?

PAINTING OF EUROPA AND ZEUS FROM A GREEK VASE

WALL PAINTING OF A MINOAN WOMAN

60. Ancient Greece has produced many great philosophers and thinkers who virtually laid down the intellectinal foundation of western civilization. Socrates was one of them. Why is he so famous?

61. Who was Plato?

62. Who was Aristotle?

63. Who was Alexander's father?

64. When did Alexander become king of Macedonia?

65. How vast was Alexander's empire?

66. When did Alexander die?

67. Who founded Rome?

68. What was the source of Rome's strength and supremacy?

69. The Roman citizens were divided into two classes, the rich and powerful, and the other commoners. What were these two classes called?

70. Who declared himself Emperor of Rome in 27BC and took the title of Augustus?

71. Who of all the generals of Rome was the greatest?

72. Besides patricians and plebians, there was another class of non-citizens in the Roman society. Who comprised this class?

73. How were the slaves treated in Rome?

74. When did Christianily become the official religion of Rome?

75. By what name was the Eastern Roman Empire known?

76. When did Rome's long hegemony and rule end?

77. Who were Assyrians?

78. Which were the capitals of Assyria?

79. Who were celts?

80. Which were the ancient American civilizations?

STATUE OF THE EMPORER AUGUSTUS

STATUE OF ASSYRIAN KING ASHURNASIRPAL II

Chapter 11

1. One of the ancient civilizaitons of the world known as a Mesopotamian or Sumerian civilization developed between the rivers Tigris and Euphrates in about 5000 BC.

2. Ur and Uruk were 2 famous Sumerian cities.

STONE STATUE OF A SUMERIAN
TEMPLE OFFICIAL

SARGON OF AKKAD CONQUERED THE WHOLE OF SUMER AND AKKAD CREATING THE WORLD'S FIRST EMPIRE

3. The most important contribution of Sumerians was the invention of writing.

4. Cuneiform means wedge shaped. It was the Sumerian system of writing. They used symbols and made them of clay tablets with wedge shaped pens. These wedgeshaped strokes represented words.

5. At the centre of all the Sumerian activities was a temple. The Sumerians worshipped many gods and goddesses.

6. The ancient Sumerian cities can be identified with modern state of Iraq.

7. There were constant attacks on Sumer by the Akkadians and Elamites. They defeated the Sumerians and created their own empire.

KING
HAMMURABI

8. Hammurabi has been most famous of all the kings of Babylon. He is well known for his strict legal code and its practical application.

9. The famous gardens of Babylon were called the Hanging Gardens.

10. In ancient Egypt the kings were called 'Pharaohs' which meant 'Great House'.

11. An Egyptian king often married a sister or half-sister to keep the royal blood pure.

12. The Sphinx and Pyramids were raised for the burial of kings, queens and other royal personalities. These are great tombs in the memory of these rulers. Their dead bodies were mummified and laid down at rest within these monuments.

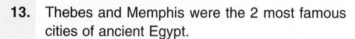

GOLDEN FUNERAL MASK OF THE EGYPTIAN BOY-KING, TUTANKHAMUN

13. Thebes and Memphis were the 2 most famous cities of ancient Egypt.

14. The river Nile has ever been life-blood of Egypt. In ancient days the river watered vast plains and increased their fertility and the whole country grew rich and prosperous. The Egyptians cultivated the land for thousand of years.

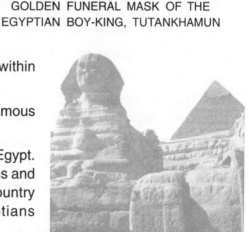

15. Persian kings ruled over Egypt during 525-404 BC.

THE STONE MONUMENT OF THE GREAT SPHINX IN EGYPT

16. Alexander the Great conqured Egypt in 332 BC.

17. After Alexander, his general Ptolemy and his successor ruled over Egypt.

18. Egypt became part of the Roman Empire in 30 BC.

19. Cleopatra was the beautiful queen of Egypt who ruled until the Roman conquest of Egypt by Julius Caesar in 30 BC. She had a love-affair with Caesar. She was last of the Ptolemies. She ultimately committed suicide after the defeat of Mark Anthony the successor of Julius Caesar.

CLEOPATRA

20. Hieroglyphics was the Egyption system of picture writing in ancient days. Hieroglyph means a picture. Each hieroglyph stood for a picture. There were series of pictures which conveyed a particular message.

21. A mummy is a dead body preserved by means of a process called mummification. In ancient Egypt dead bodies of kings, queens and other royal persons were preserved. Their internal organs were removed, the bodies dried, oiled, spiced, wrapped in linen and then put into coffins.

22. Early civilization grew up in the Indus Valley. These two cities were centres of this ancient civilization. They had their own system of writing and governance. A number of beautiful seals have been found at Harappa and Mohenjodaro which throw ample light on the 5000 year old Indian civilization.

INDUS VALLEY POT

23. The early Aryans settled in the east Punjab between the river Satluz and Yamuna, and along the upper course of Saraswati, now extinct.

24. The Aryans came to India between 2000 BC and 1500 BC.

25. The Rig Veda is the earliest source of ancient Indian culture and life. The other Vedas are Yajur Veda, Sam Veda and Atharva Veda.

26. The most important difference between the two ancient civilizations is that the Indus Valley civilization was urban and the Aryan civilization was rural and pastoral.

27. The Aryans proved far superior in military might because of their horse driven chariots and weapons of bronze.

28. The Ramyana and the Mahabharata are 2 most famous epics of India.

29. The decline and fall of the Indus Valley civilization should have begun by 2000 BC. Either there were unprecedented floods in the river Indus or some such other devastation which caused the fall and destruction of this great civilization. Some are of the opinion that the Aryan invasion destroyed this mighty civilization.

INDUS VALLEY TOYS

30. King Bimbsara founded the mighty empire of Magadha.

31. Gautama Buddha was born in the Lumbani forest near Kkapilvastu. He belonged to the Shakyas and was the son of King Suddhodhana.

32. Buddha means 'enlightened' and 'awakened one.'.

33. Alexander invaded India is 326 BC.

34. Porus, the king of Punjab put up tough resistance against Alexander but was defeated.

35. Chandra Gupta Maurya was an Indian king who rose to great heights after Alexander's attack on India.

36. Chanyka was a great diplomat and politician. He was Chandragupta Maurya's guru and chief adviser.

37. The two other wellknown names of Chanakya are— Kautilya and Vishnugupta.

38. Seleucus Nicator, a general of Alaxander, entered into matrimonial alliance with Chandragupta Maurya by giving him his daughter in marriage.

39. Ashoka was son of king Bindusara. Ashoka succeeded him in 273 BC and proved a great emperor and administrator.

LIONS AT THE TOP OF ONE OF ASHOKA'S PILLARS

40. Ashoka became a stauch Buddhist after the war of Kalinga. The miseries and sufferings of the war melted the heart of Ashoka and so he resolved never to wage war or commit violence.

41. Ashoka sent missionaries to other countries and exhorted his own subjects to follow the dharma. He got many edicts erected and engraved to preach the ethics of Buddhism.

42. Ashokan empire encompassed almost all the sub-continent except some parts in the south.

43. King Samudragupta restored Patliputra to its former glory and splendour.

44. Under Chandragupta II Hindu India achieved the Golden Age.

45. Chandragupta II was popularly known as Chandragupta Vikrmaditya. His name is associated with Vikram Era.

46. The Vikram Era began in 58 BC.

47. Kalidas, a great poet dramatist and author of Shakuntala, Meghdoot etc. lived in Chardragupta Vikramaditya's court.

STATUE OF THE GOD VISHNU FROM THE GUPTA PERIOD

48. The court language of the Guptas was Sanskrit.

49. The ancient Greek civilization began about 4000 years ago.

50. We owe many things to the great Greek civilization. Their contribution to literature art, philosophy, mathematies, institution of democracy, architecture, theatre and games has been really outstanding.

51. Athens and Sparta were the most famous city states of ancient Greece.

52. The gods and goddesses of ancient Greeks lived on Mount Olympus.

53. The golden period of ancient Greek civilizaiton is known as the Classical Period.

54. The Spartans were welknown for their fearlessness, strict discipline and qualities of brave warriors.

55. Homer was the author of Iliad and Odyssey, the two great Greek epics.

56. It is known as Minon Civilization after king Minos of Knosses. It spread to Mycenae on the mainland and flourished for long.

57. Marathon was a place in ancient Greece where King Darius of Persia was defeated by

A GREEK PRINCE CALLED THESEUS PREPARES TO KILL THE MINOTAUR, A HALF-BULL AND HALF-MAN

Athenious in 491BC. A greek athlete and runner had to cover the distance of 26 miles to carry the news of victory of Athens. The modern Marathon in athletics is a long distance endurance race of 26 miles in memory of this ancient event.

58. Sport formed an important part of Greek civilization as a means of entertainment and keeping physically fit and mentally alert. There were held many local and national games and sports.

59. Olympic Games were held every four years at Olympia. They were held for five days in honour of Zeus, the god of gods. The winners became national heroes and fame and fortune attended them.

60. Socrates (469-399BC) was a son of an Athenian sculptor. He was one of the greatest ancient thinkers of Greece. He taught people the ethics of good and evil. But some politicians did not approve his thinking and so he was forced to die by consuming poison.

61. Plato(427-348BC) was the author of the famous book Republic in which he describes an ideal way of governance and adminstration. He ran a famous academy near Athens and tought his student about morals, ethics and politics.

62. Aristotle (384-322BC) was another great philosopher of Greece. He was the teacher and tutor of Alexander the Great. His ideas and thinking on logic are still held quite relevant in the modern philosophy.

63. King Philip II of Macedonia was Alexander's father. He consolidated his power by defeating Persians and uniting the Macedonians and Greeks.

STATUE OF ALEXANDER WEARING A LION SKIN

64. Alexander the Great became king of Macedonia after the death of his father Philip II in 336 BC. Then Alexander was 20 yeas old.

65. Alexander's empire was the largest in the ancient world. It extended from Greece in the west to India in the east. He conquered whole of the Persia and became its unrivalled king.

66. Alexander died in 323 BC at young age of 32 while retreating from India to Babylon.

67. Rome was founded by Romulus and Remus. The legend says that they were brought up by a she-wolf.

68. The source of Rome's strength and military supremacy was its huge and very disciplined army. The Roman soldiers mainly fought on foot with their long spears and broad round shields.

69. The two classes were called Particians and the Plebians. The first consisted of a few rich, privileged and powerful people and the second consisted of common, poor and underprivileged people.

70. In 27 BC Octavian declared himself the Emperor of Rome and took the title of Augustus. Originally Rome was a Republic and ruled by a powerful Senate, but Octavian became so powerful as a general that he defeated another general Brutus and declared himself an emperor.

71. Julius Caesar was the greatest of all the Roman generals. He became famous for his great wars and victories. But later he was murdered by another general named Brutus because Caesar had become a dictator.

72. Provincials, who lived outside Rome but in lands under Rome, and the slaves comprised the non-citizens.

73. Slaves were treated cruelly. They had to perform very hard work and most menial duties. They were owned by wealthy citizens or the government.

74. In 291 AD Christianity became the official religion of Rome.

75. The Eastern Roman Empire was known as Byzantine Empire.

76. Rome's long hegemony and rule ended in 410AD when barbarian invaders sacked Rome.

77. The Assyrians originally lived around the river Tigris but gradually they grew very mighty in about 2000 BC and had many warrior kings.

78. Assyria had three capitals one after the other. The first was Ashur. The second capital was Nimrud. The third and last was Nineveh. The three different kings chose these three cities as their different capitals.

79. Celts were tribal people who lived in France and Austria during 600-500 BC. They were fearlers wariors and ruthless fighters. But at last they were defeated by the Romans in 225 BC. Many tribes lived individually and had built big fortresses on tops of the hills.

80. The Olmecs and the Chavin were two ancient civilizations of America. The Olmecs grew up is the central America from about 1200 BC in western Mexico. The Chavin civilization grew up along the coast of northern Peru. Their forefathers had migrated from Asia thousands of years before.

SOME FAMOUS SCIENTISTS

Michael Faraday

A. Leeuwen Hoek

Henry Cavendish

James Watt

Claude Bernard

Charles Darwin

Lamarck

Gregor Mendel

Copernicus

Baird

Louis Pasteur

Sir Isaac Newton

Edward Jenner

Galileo Galilie